A Friendly Life

THE AUTOBIOGRAPHY OF S. PRESTLEY BLAKE
CO-FOUNDER OF FRIENDLY ICE CREAM CORP.

by S. Prestley Blake
with Alan Farnham

BRIGANTINE MEDIA

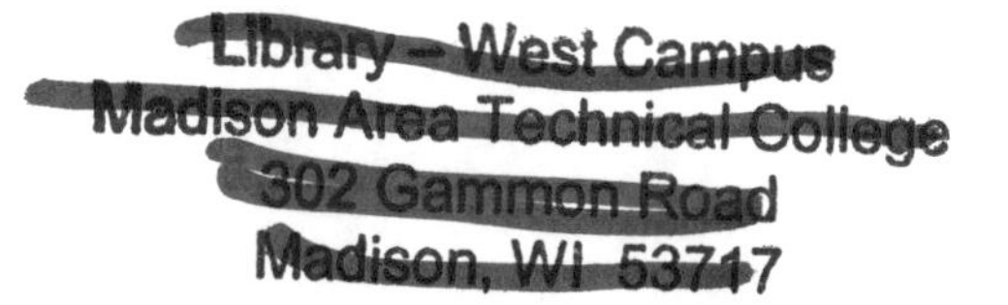

A Friendly Life

Published by Brigantine Media
211 North Ave., St. Johnsbury, Vermont 05819

Cover and Book Design by Jacob L. Grant

ISBN 978-0-9826644-1-4

For more information on these books please contact:
Brigantine Media
211 North Avenue, St. Johnsbury, Vermont 05819
Phone: 802-751-8802
Email: neil@brigantinemedia.com
Website: www.brigantinemedia.com

For Mr. and Mrs. Herbert P. Blake,
my parents,
who gave us the help we needed
to start our business.

A special thank you to Rose Slate.

Table of Contents

FOREWORD

YOU NEVER HAVE TO WONDER HOW PRES BLAKE FEELS ABOUT an issue or person, or whether that person is speaking the truth, or whether money is more important than values to him. You do have to worry if Pres Blake feels you have violated business ethics or deceived or taken advantage of those you have an obligation to protect.

Blake is an avenger with the persistence of a pit bull—all in the pursuit of fairness and justice for the little guy, particularly when up against Goliath. Pres is a Lone Ranger, a straight arrow, a Sherlock Holmes, a hard-charging fullback, a bulldozer, and one tough cookie—all contained in a large frame, with a stern voice and a mind-set calculated to make you realize the seriousness of your transgression.

Imagine the mistake Don Smith, Chairman and CEO of Friendly Ice Cream Corporation, made when trying to stonewall, deceive, and bully Pres Blake. Blake's anger went into overdrive when he saw the damage being done to the reputation and image of the company he and his brother founded almost 75 years earlier. This is the true story of a retired, successful businessman who became concerned that Smith was harming Friendly's employees, shareholders, and community.

Pres had left Friendly's management in 1979, when he sold the company to Hershey, who later sold to Smith. When Smith took Friendly's public, he opened the door to review and examination. Pres did not like what he saw one bit, and the battle began. I was pleased to be the catalyst who urged Pres to take concrete action to stop the damage being done to his former company and employees. It was at my suggestion that he began purchasing a large block of shares.

Blake bought 12% of the Friendly stock to fire his first shot across the bow of Smith and Smith's errant board and spent hundreds of thousands of dollars for legal services to investigate the out-of-touch directors. He then joined forces with newly found allies who worked with Blake to save the company, its jobs, and its market value.

You know you've got a strong and meaningful story to tell when Harvard Business School writes it up into one of their famous case studies. It's an ethics and human relations study that illustrates the virtue of upholding fair and honest business dealing over a greed-fueled grab for a quick buck.

This book is about Pres Blake's life and values. It is also a view into the type of people and the unethical behavior that are presently devastating the world economy. Massive egos, short cuts, deceit, and illegal actions are principal causes of our nation's present precarious economic position.

Thank goodness Pres hasn't had to wrestle with skunks his entire life. He's enjoyed himself. He's sailed the seas, traveled the world, met the great and near-great. He's logged enough adventures for two lifetimes. In this book you'll share those adventures and meet some of the most admirable people in the world. I envy you your experience!

Lyman Wood

Lyman Wood, for forty years a leading citizen of the New England business community, earned his MBA from Harvard in 1961. He has owned and operated companies, served as a senior executive, and has chaired the boards of numerous non-profits. He remains active in philanthropy.

FLASHBACK: MAY 2001

A HUSH FELL OVER THE AUDITORIUM WHERE THE STOCKHOLDERS of Friendly Ice Cream gathered for their annual meeting on May 16, 2001.

Notebook pages rustled as financial reporters, smuggled into the session as stockholder "guests" (in defiance of a news blackout imposed by management), flipped to a new page. Brokers, bankers, and Friendly's shareholders, many of them retirees, twisted their necks to see a tall, robust, white-haired man rise from his seat.

He waved away the microphone, and with a clear voice began to ask a list of simple questions that were body blows to Friendly's management:

Why was a company drowning in debt paying for its part-time CEO to flit around the country on a pricey corporate jet? Why was that same CEO, Donald Smith, diverting Friendly's resources to benefit a separate restaurant chain—Perkins—of which he owned 70%?

"You're out of order," barked Smith, a brusque, hard-driving, former Burger King executive with a proclivity for using four-letter words. "Sit down, sit down."

"When I am finished," replied the man, in tones as icy as the frozen desserts served by the 500-restaurant chain. He hammered home the rest of his pointed questions, refusing to be silenced.

This was no obscure dissident who had risen to wail and scold like Dickens's Ghost of Christmas Past. It was S. Prestley Blake, Friendly's patriarch and co-founder. More than two decades after selling Friendly's for $164 million, Blake, at 86, had come roaring back, scooping up 12% of Friendly's plummeting stock—870,000 shares—in a matter of a few weeks, emerging as Friendly's biggest shareholder. The cost had been nearly two million dollars, all of it from Blake's own pocket.

"I did it to get attention," he told newsmen, a mischievous glint in his eye. "I figured the company would listen to their largest stockholder. It would only be polite."

He was determined, he said, to get to the bottom of what had gone wrong with the restaurant chain he had devoted 43 years of his life to building. Employee morale was terrible; the stock was sinking; talent was heading for the door. Meanwhile management seemed to be more interested in lining its own pockets than in addressing, let alone solving, the company's problems.

Powerless though Smith might be to silence Blake, he was determined not to answer him at this meeting or any subsequent one.

So Blake filed a freedom-of-information lawsuit. It was round one of what was to become a very public battle between two powerful businessmen for the company's soul. At an age when most men are content to play golf and bask in retirement, Blake was gunning for justice.

Introduction

WHY I GOT UP OFF THE COUCH

ALLOW ME, PLEASE, TO INTRODUCE MYSELF: I'M PRES BLAKE. I was that angry shareholder. Did I want to go to court? Did I want to come out of a comfortable retirement and, at age 86, get all suited up again for a fight? No. I was in good health, with no worries to speak of and plenty of money in the bank. I had—and still have—a wonderful wife. I had two nice homes, a yacht, a barn full of vintage Rolls-Royces, and enough grandkids to keep me on my toes. In fact, the title of this chapter is misleading, now that I think about it. I wasn't on the couch. I was enjoying life to its fullest. I was busy. I've got eleven diesel tractors working right now at my summer place, doing landscaping. So, it's not exactly that I was sitting around eating bonbons.

I'd already had plenty of aggravation in the course of my career—you can't very well avoid it in this life, if you're going to be a go-getter and try to build something—a business, or anything else. I wasn't hankering for more. Sometimes, however, you have to do what's right, whether it suits your convenience or not. I felt an obligation to save my company, the one I'd built and loved—"my baby," the Friendly Ice Cream Corporation—from being run into the ground by a pack of spendthrift managers more intent on lining their own pockets than on giving the public good hamburgers, good shakes, and good service. It seemed clear to me that if this bunch stayed in power, Friendly's stock, which had already tumbled from $18 a share in 1997 to less than $2 a share in 2001, would be worth practically nothing. Small investors, many of them retired Friendly's employees who'd put their life savings in the stock, would be left high and dry.

I guess you can see I'm stubborn. Always have been. To do nothing when you see a wrong being committed—well, that's just not how I was raised. So, after consulting with my wife Helen and some friends, I decided to jump in. And when I jump into something, I do it with both feet. Little did I know then how many years the fight would take or how much money it would cost. If somebody had told me back then that the whole thing would wind up taking five years and cost almost eleven million dollars, including legal fees—or, for that matter, that the whole adventure would be taught today as a case study in shareholder activism at the Harvard Business School—well, I'd have said, "Friend, your cone is dripping."

Who won, who lost, and why it matters now are the subjects of this book. It's quite a tale, if I do say so myself, and I hope that you enjoy it. But that's not all you'll find here. I'm also going to tell the story of how my brother and I, starting with no more money than what you've got in your pocket right now, set out during the worst of the Great Depression to start our little ice cream business. I'll tell you how much fun that was; what kind of challenges we faced; how we learned and grew and overcame them. I'll especially enjoy sharing with you all the good things that came along with that hard work: the trips around the world and the yachts and Rolls-Royces; the famous people I met; the "big" men of business who took an interest in me and helped me ("big" because they were not just successful but generous and open-hearted). But before I get too far ahead of myself, I'm going to do a favor for you that business schools do for their students: I'm going to give you my book's executive summary. That's sort of a cheat sheet that tries to get across, at the very outset, the point of what the writer has to say. As far as I'm concerned, the story you'll find here has four morals.

First, start out thinking small and working hard. The big dreams come later. When we started our business it was just my brother and me. We had no thoughts of a second store, let alone a 500-store chain. We just were two guys starting an ice cream store, and we weren't afraid to work hard at it, literally day and night.

Second, don't be afraid to ask other people for advice. My brother and I couldn't have started our business without our parents. They put in the initial capital, and we lived at home. Talk about a family business. Our business was our family.

As we grew, we worked with other people. Our business grew and prospered because of the people we hired and trained. And as our business started to take off, we found other businessmen, like J.C. Penney and General Motors CEOs Harlow Curtice and Tom Murphy, who were happy to help keep us on the right course.

Third, after you achieve some success, you have to dream and live big. Once you get over the initial hump, you have to take your idea and run with it. And never stop. There's always another challenge. Whether it's going to the North Pole or sailing a yacht up the Gambia River, I've never shied away from an adventure.

Fourth, give back. I've been a lucky guy. My brother and I had loving parents, good health, ambition, and self-discipline. Those were my advantages. Success in business, in the courtroom, and in life came to me mainly because of these. I always remember I came from an ordinary background. That's why I give to schools and libraries. I want to help other people who are looking for the tools to do well in life.

I'm grateful for the opportunities I've had in life. And it all started because I couldn't get a job in Springfield...

PART 1

Building *Friendly* Ice Cream

SPRINGFIELD

SPRINGFIELD, MASSACHUSETTS, WHERE I WAS BORN, WAS made of opportunity.

In the 1920s, a little kid like me could look around and see all the local places where innovators of every sort had found success. It was in Springfield, for example, that Horace Smith met up with Daniel Wesson in the 1850s, and the two had gone on to found gun maker Smith & Wesson. In 1891 James Naismith, a physical education teacher at Springfield College, invented something more benign—basketball. And two years after that, a pair of brothers named Duryea began manufacturing the first gasoline-powered car sold in the United States.

Other makers of vehicles and parts (the high tech industries of their day) were drawn to Springfield by its expanding nucleus of tinkerers, metal workers, skilled mechanics, and engineers. Indian Motorcycles started business here in 1901.

In 1921, when I was seven, Rolls-Royce chose Springfield as its one and only U.S. site for making chassis. Their plant, which was located close to the junior high school I attended, sent 3,000 Silver Ghosts and Phantoms out into the world, and we kids "ooohed" and "aaahed" as each zoomed past.

The plant built only chassis. The bodies were put on elsewhere. Company policy decreed that each chassis had to be driven 100 miles before its body could be added. We would watch the test drives of these Rolls-Royces, naked of everything except a bucket seat, as their drivers went zipping around the city. I guess it's not surprising that with this kind of introduction to these marvelous machines, I'd later wind up owning several dozen of them as an adult, once I'd earned some money. It was the beginning of my lifelong love affair with fine cars, which continues to this day.

The plant closed in 1931 never to reopen—like so many others a casualty of the Great Depression. By my late teens, people everywhere in Springfield were out of work. They didn't have money for life's necessities, let alone Rolls-Royces.

There were just no jobs to be had, especially if you were young. Experts estimated that nationwide during the Great Depression 40% of people aged 16 to 24 who were not in school were unemployed.

Despair sucked the life out of people, both rich and poor.

The rich, who'd lost money in the stock market crash, jumped out of windows. The poor scrounged around in alleys.

My dad, Herbert Blake, managed to stay employed even during the worst of this. His job, vice president for sales at the Standard Electric Time Company, required him to travel, but it kept our family afloat: my mother Ethel, me, my brother Curtis, and our little sister Betsy. Another sibling, Hollis, had died at the age of two. We didn't have luxuries, but on the other hand, we didn't want for a comfortable home or warm clothes or good food. By the standards of the times, we were doing well.

From my perspective, the summer of 1935 was the trough of the Depression. It seemed impossible that things could get worse. If there weren't jobs for adults, you can be sure there weren't any summer jobs for Curt and me (then 18 and 20, respectively). When we tried to get work pumping gas, the station owner turned us down flat: he already had more applications than he could count from college graduates!

Neither Curt nor I had been very keen on college. I'd spent a year at Trinity College in Hartford, but found it hard to keep my mind on my courses. The college didn't teach the one subject that really interested me—business. Curt logged a year at Duke, but he didn't like it any better than I had Trinity. He did it, I think, only to please our father. Both our parents were college graduates. They believed in education, and I think they were disappointed not to see either of us graduate.

Curt's and my situation that summer presented our folks with something of a problem: if we weren't going to continue with college, and if there weren't any jobs, what, exactly, were we going to do? While I'm sure they wanted us to make money, it was more important to them that we have something to keep us off the streets and out of trouble.

Enter Mom. To Ethel Blake, a banker's daughter and schoolteacher, the solution was obvious: if her sons couldn't find jobs working for somebody else, then they'd have to work for themselves. So she was more than a little interested one day to hear about a man across town who had bought a freezer on the installment plan, opened up a little shop, and was selling ice cream that he made right in his own store. Why couldn't her sons do the same?

While my dad was on a business trip to Dallas that June of 1935, he got a letter from my mother outlining her plans for a "business for the boys." That our dad quickly agreed to her idea may have had something to do with the fact that I had already shown him that I had a pretty good head for business.

My first business, which I ran when I was 12, was a newspaper route of 125 customers who were on five or six streets. I soon saw how to make it more efficient: I traded some of my customers with those of another boy, Charlie Godin, whose route also covered five or six streets. The result was that all my customers were now lined up along a single street, Massachusetts Avenue, just one street over from where I lived. Instead of hopscotching blocks, all I had to do was run my bicycle up one side and down the other. I made about $3 a week, and by the time I was 16 I'd saved $25—enough to buy a Model T Ford. You can be sure I never drove it on Massachusetts Avenue: I didn't want my customers getting the idea that I was doing so well they didn't have to tip me!

My dad also recognized my ambition in my drive to become an Eagle Scout. I worked hard after school on my merit badges, and reached my goal in my early teens. My father knew that few boys attained that distinction.

So it was decided. Curt and I would start our own business. It was the worst of times for the American economy, but it turned out to be just the right time for two hardworking young men to get started.

TWO FRIENDLY GUYS

IT COST MY PARENTS PRECISELY $547 TO PUT THEIR SONS ON the road to becoming ice cream barons. The "baron" part would have made them laugh. I don't think either one of them expected us to stick with our little business any longer than through the summer. I don't think they expected to get their principal back. It was strictly a make-work project to give us an alternative to bank robbing (that's a joke) and keep us from falling in with the wrong crowd (that's not). The money covered our down payment for the freezer and our rental of a storefront at 161 Boston Road. Neither of us was of legal age yet, so my mother signed the lease and all the other legal papers.

We now faced our first challenge: what to call the business?

My brother came up with the name: "Friendly Ice Cream." We were two friendly guys, he reasoned, and we wanted our little store to be a friendly place. We couldn't afford to have a sign made, so

I made one from letters I cut out of wood. It cost us $16 and it still hangs today at Friendly's corporate headquarters. (In fact, in 2001 it was trotted out and prominently displayed at the infamous shareholders' meeting at the start of this book—the one where Smith and I had our first public unpleasantness.)

We picked up eight wooden chairs and a couple of tables at a used furniture shop for $8. We installed the ice cream freezer and a Coca-Cola cooler. And as fast as you can say, "One scoop or two?" we were in business!

We opened the afternoon of July 18, 1935.

The local newspaper said the temperature was in the 90s—a good day if you're selling ice cream. We had customers immediately, and it wasn't any mystery to understand why: we charged less. The bigger ice cream stores charged a dime for two scoops. We charged a nickel. And our quality was better.

Was I scared when I first stepped behind the counter? Not in the slightest. In our minds, we weren't launching some big enterprise. We were just a couple of guys keeping busy for the summer.

I don't remember who was the first person to pay five cents for one of our double-dip cones. Over the years many people have told me they were our first customer.

That day's receipts? I remember them vividly: $27.61.

Sales next day plummeted to $20.

Did we care? No! We were having a wonderful adventure!

Our mother kept the books, such as they were. Men's shirts, in those days, came from the laundry folded around stiff cardboard. She'd take those cardboard sheets, rule them off in columns, one for each day of the week, and use these to record daily total receipts and cash payouts. That wasn't her only contribution to the business. Her favorite ice cream flavor was coffee. To make sure we'd always have it, she brewed coffee syrup in her own kitchen percolator. The other flavors we sold were what you'd expect: vanilla, chocolate, strawberry, and a few others. My favorites are still chocolate and coffee.

As Dad traveled, he kept track of our financials, scribbling notes on hotel stationery. His critique of projected expenses arrived written on notepaper from the Hotel Edison in New York City. An analysis of the cost of raw materials bore the logo of the Benjamin Franklin Hotel in Philadelphia. His first estimate of profit (income $540, expenses $419, dated June 23, 1935) arrived tucked into an envelope from the William Penn Hotel in Houston, whose letterhead trumpeted the fact that the Penn was "completely air conditioned."

Those first days, our work never seemed to end. We opened at 11:00 in the morning and didn't close until 11:00 at night—or later, if we could see another nickel customer coming down the street. One brother stayed to clean up and make the ice cream for the next day, not getting home until 5:00 in the morning. He'd catch a few hours sleep, then return around 2:00 in the afternoon. The other would open the shop. We traded off working the late shift. There was no such thing as a day off.

It was an exhausting, nerve-wracking grind, and after two weeks of it, we had our first argument: who would do the dishes?

"You do them," I told Curt. He shot back, "I did them last night."

One thing led to another, and it grew into a pretty big fight. I don't remember who did the dishes, but they got done.

Next morning, after the dust had settled, I said, "You know, Curt, if we are going to make a success of this, we can never again have an argument over such a stupid thing as who's going to do the dishes. Let's set up a system so we know who's doing the dishes which night." It was the first and only business argument we ever had while we were running Friendly.

The flare-up over dishes was also the first time in our partnership that I laid down the law. I didn't realize it at the time, but I was starting to take charge and assert my leadership.

When we eventually incorporated, we flipped a coin to decide who would be president. Curt won. He was president and I was treasurer and in charge of purchasing and real estate. It took me a long time to realize that, regardless of title, I was the real boss by temperament, and Curt knew it. Henry Ford had never been president of Ford Motor Company. He was treasurer and Edsel was president. If being treasurer was good enough for Henry Ford, it was good enough for me.

Our modest success did not go unnoticed by the biggest ice cream store in town, which fought back by cutting its prices in half to compete with ours. There was an immediate loss of customers wanting the discount cones. Our sales fell, and we were worried. But the big store's strategy worked too well: they attracted so many customers there were long lines and a long wait for service. Pretty soon those customers gave up waiting and returned to us, where they could pay the same price and skip the inconvenience.

As summer gave way to fall, we began to appreciate that we had a good thing going. But soon our customers would be thinking more about skidding on ice than eating it, however creamy. If we were going to nurse the business through the winter we'd need to offer something more than ice cream. What else should we serve? We decided to ask. We put out pencils and little slips of paper so our customers could vote on what they'd prefer to have—hamburgers or hot dogs. Hamburgers won handily. Later on, we added toasted cheese sandwiches to accommodate Catholic customers who wanted an alternative to meat on Fridays.

On this occasion and many others, customers turned out to be our best advisers. More than once they disabused us of wrong-headed notions.

When you're scooping ice cream, it's inevitable that every now and then a drip will fall on the counter. That gave me a bright idea! Why not just leave them there? I figured customers would see the drippings and think to themselves, "These two guys are doing such a heck of a business they can't keep up." One day a woman came into the store, took one look at our counter with all its dribbles, and said, "My, how messy." Wow! Did I ever learn my lesson! From that day forward, our counter was pristine.

Another lesson? Picture this: I'm serving an ice cream cone. The customer hands it to her little boy, and the kid drops it. All of a sudden, the kid is standing there crying. I give him another ice cream cone, and everyone in the store watches the smile spread across his face. For the cost of an ice cream cone—not even the nickel, just the wholesale cost—I've made all these people happy. The kid's tears stop. He licks his cone. Goodwill prevails! This became the model for how we wanted all our customers to be treated. Later on, as Friendly grew, we taught it to all our managers: replace a dropped cone with no argument. Don't even think about trying to charge for a replacement cone! This was part of a larger philosophy: never try to pull any fast ones on customers, to gouge them or shortchange them.

Despite our menu expansion, receipts declined as the days got shorter and colder. Some days all we'd take in would be $16. And that was with our working 12 hours a day or sometimes more. We were discouraged. All we were allowing ourselves in pay was $4 a week each. I remember once telling Curt, "You know, a friend of ours just got a job working for the telephone company for $14 a week. Shouldn't we chuck this and go get a job like that?" Maybe we should have. But it was still the Depression and neither of us could find a job like that, so we stuck with what we had, barely managing to make payments on the freezer and pay our rent.

I didn't realize this until many years later, but the reason we were able to keep our little business limping along—and the only reason Curt and I could live on $4 a week—was that we both still lived at home. We didn't have wives. We didn't have families to support. We didn't have to pay for room and board.

Ordinarily a person starting his own business has to draw a living wage, for food and clothing and a place for his family to live. If the business can't pay those costs, and often when it's new it can't, he has to borrow. Then there's the added cost of interest to be paid. Even if he buys an existing business that's producing $100,000 a year, half of that typically will have to go to pay off his loan, and the other half to support his family.

That wasn't our situation at all. Many weeks, the only thing I'd spend any money on would be a 5-cent candy bar.

It's for this reason that I say that neither one of us was an entrepreneur. We didn't take any gamble. We didn't put anything at risk, except our time. What little money we invested in growing the business came directly out of profits. We didn't borrow. For the first five years of Friendly Ice Cream, that's how our business survived. It's not that we were such brilliant businessmen. We worked hard and lived economically. It's not a bad way to get a business started.

PROGRESS BY BABY STEPS

DURING OUR FIRST WINTER IN BUSINESS, CURT AND I discovered that the car we'd been depending on as our utility vehicle—a 1928 Model A Ford touring car we had bought used for $40—had begun to fail us. We needed something more reliable, and I'd found a candidate I thought was excellent: a new $620 Ford Phaeton touring car in Washington blue. It could be ours, said the salesman, for a down payment of $25.

I couldn't wait to tell Dad and Curt about this terrific deal. True, it entailed a $129 finance charge, but the Ford dealership was offering us $115 more for our decrepit Model A than it had cost.

Probably the biggest endorsement we ever got from Dad was his approval of this purchase. He gave the matter considerable thought, then said he thought we were doing well enough to justify the $25 monthly payment. He saw that buying the car would boost our morale. To us, it was the first real evidence of our success.

I still remember the cold night I picked it up and drove it home. It was an absolute thrill—more, ever so much more, than taking possession of any other car I ever bought, even a custom-built Rolls-Royce. I can remember how the Phaeton's headlights reflected off the snowbanks piled on either side of the road. When I got to the store, I parked right in front so the car would be illuminated by the bright blue and yellow of our neon "Friendly Ice Cream" window sign.

Curt, seeing the spectacle, threw off his apron and jumped the counter. He was off duty and I was on. He drove for miles and miles before returning.

Over the next 75 years we owned many beautiful cars. But never, in Curt's life or mine, would we ever own one as thrilling, as spectacular, or as rich in significance as this one.

A year later we made another decision. We repaid our parents' $547 investment with interest—$600. Curt and I had about $2,000 in the company checking account by that time, so we decided we could afford it. Neither of our parents said anything—they weren't extravagant with their praise where we were concerned—but I like to think that when they went to bed that night, they were proud of us.

After a few years, I began thinking about opening a second store. I found a location that I liked in West Springfield. The cost of a second store worked out to about $18,000. We would need a bank loan of $10,000, and the balance would come from the money we had saved.

Expansion to a second store presented us with new challenges and opportunities. For the first time, we would have to hire a store manager. Planning a new store gave us the opportunity to determine how we wanted it to look. There, as in our subsequent stores, we decided all food preparation should be in plain view of customers, so they could come away impressed by our high standards of cleanliness.

Our second store opened at 7:00 pm on November 14, 1940, and it was a hit from the start. As far as we could see, the future for Friendly looked bright.

Those first five years, with our first and second stores, were a prelude to all that was to follow. Our success, though modest, confirmed our belief that customers would keep coming back if a few simple but high-quality items were offered at a fair price and served by cheerful, courteous people.

For quality control we trusted our own palates and stomachs, as well as those of our customers, who continued to give us invaluable feedback. We could see with our own eyes, day by day, how small refinements and improvements in our methods led to more money in the cash register.

We got really good at making ice cream. The secret to ice cream is using the very freshest cream with just the right amount of butterfat: the more fat, the richer the flavor. Too much fat, though, and the ice cream will be too rich for most customers' taste.

We bought hamburger at the market next door. It arrived fresh daily in ten-pound packets. Curt and I would open each one and cook a little sample as a test. We would taste it and smell it, of course. But we also learned to take a little pinch and rub it between our fingers, because meat that's been around too long gets a slippery feel. If the meat failed any of our tests, back it went. Like ice cream, the amount of fat related directly to the flavor: too little, and there was hardly any taste; too much, and the burgers would be greasy and shrink on the grill.

The lessons of these early years never left us.

We avoided debt like the plague, fueling almost all our growth from profits. On rare occasions when we did borrow, we repaid our loans as quickly as possible. If that meant we grew more slowly than we otherwise might have, that was fine by us. We paid our bills fast, which enabled us to get one or two percent off for prompt payment. Maybe that sounds corny or old fashioned, but it's the philosophy that carried us through 43 years of running Friendly Ice Cream.

CLOSED FOR THE WAR

JUST OVER A YEAR AFTER WE OPENED OUR SECOND STORE, World War II changed everything. The war up-ended life for us, our customers, and our employees.

The war didn't catch us completely by surprise. It had been clear to anybody with eyes and ears that the days of U.S. neutrality were numbered. Still, no one had expected Japan to attack.

At first, Curt and I did not recognize that war meant we'd have to close our stores. But as our employees and customers began to enlist or be drawn into war work, we eventually bowed to the inevitable. Curt was single and he enlisted in the Army Air Corps.

I was married by then and had a baby daughter, so I was ineligible for the draft. Still, I wanted to do my part. I decided I could make the biggest contribution to the war effort by putting my business skills to work as an expediter: someone who finds and hurries along materials vital to making armaments. When I heard that the local Westinghouse plant in Springfield was looking for just such an expediter, I went after it with all my might. I got letters of recommendation from at least 15 different references—minister, customers, friends, parents, suppliers. One of the secretaries at Westinghouse later told me she had never seen such a full-court press. "We had no choice," she said. "We had to hire you!"

Once I had the job, it was clear there was no way I could help win the war and keep our stores open at the same time. So, with much regret, I closed them. I put signs in the windows:

> GONE to the SERVICE. This store will be CLOSED until we win the war. This store is NOT for rent.

"Not for rent" because we were closing temporarily, not permanently. Curt and I were absolutely of the same mind about that. Not only did we intend to reopen after the war, during the war we wrote back and forth to each other constantly, making plans for what we would do when we reopened.

My job at Westinghouse had me hunting up hard-to-find aircraft parts, including capacitors and radio equipment made in Ohio, New Jersey, and Massachusetts. Once I'd located the necessary parts, I'd hurry them along to Springfield, sometimes driving them there all night myself. I'd always been a heck of a go-getter, and that trait served me well in expediting.

That job was the only one I ever had working for someone else. After the war, a Westinghouse vice president asked me if I would stay on. I told him I was flattered, but that I couldn't accept. I had my own business to run.

Even during the war I'd found time on nights and weekends to help ensure that Friendly would be ready to start business with a bang once peace was restored. During wartime, sugar was rationed. If you were in the ice cream business, you got a certain sugar quota from the government. You couldn't sell your sugar, but selling sugar syrup (sugar cooked with water) was fine. It was one of those regulatory quirks. I saw that Friendly could make money by taking its sugar, turning it into syrup, and selling the syrup. This turned out to be a very profitable business. By war's end, I had banked $70,000, ready to be used for peacetime company expansion.

RARIN' TO GO

CURT WAS DUE TO BE RELEASED BY THE ARMY AIR CORPS right before Christmas 1945, and did I have surprises waiting for him! I had plans for expanding like crazy. We would have to build a new plant to supply all our new stores. But we had never had a proper office, and that was part of the new plan.

That Christmas, it snowed like the devil.

I picked Curt up from the airport, blindfolded him, and drove him in to our new office. Off came the blindfold! And there, before him, were three desks—one with Curt's name on it, another with mine, and one for our bookkeeper. Was he surprised!

After he got settled at home, he came back to the office and immediately got to work. The poor guy never had any kind of vacation between the military and getting back on the job at Friendly.

We reopened our two stores, as promised, in 1945 and 1946. In between, we added a third store in the Springfield suburb of Longmeadow. On top of that, I'd made a deal to open a fourth store in Thompsonville, Connecticut. After the setbacks of the war years, Friendly was on the march!

We got help from an unexpected quarter. One part of the G.I. Bill of Rights, the legislation aimed at helping returning servicemen adjust to the peacetime economy, provided $100 a month to any veteran taking on-the-job training. In effect, it subsidized any employer who hired veterans. We got many promising young men this way. One of our very first trainees, Robert Gaudrault, eventually became a president of Friendly.

We continued growing. By 1955, ten years after the war, we had over 25 Friendly stores.

During the 1950s, we met an enterprising salesman of Multimixers (milkshake mixers with 5 spindles). Friendly became one of his best customers, and he featured the company in sixteen different dairy magazines. As time went on, we became friends, and enjoyed talking business with him. The name of this salesman? Ray Kroc, the legendary businessman who soon would see the future in a small chain of fast-food restaurants owned by the McDonald brothers. We stayed in touch as Ray built the McDonald's Corporation, getting together every few years to swap war stories about the food business and compare notes about our favorite Rolls-Royce automobiles. When Ray's widow died, she left 1.5 billion dollars to the Salvation Army and many millions to other charities.

Expansion of the company meant learning to do business a whole new way.

Gone were the days when a couple of brothers, all by themselves, could oversee buying supplies, cooking, serving, and cleaning up. We had to hire managers, and that's never easy. It's hard to find people who share your same values or who go about solving problems the way you would yourself. If there was anything that put a limit on how fast we were able to expand in the 1950s, it was our difficulty finding the right people and devising a training program to make sure that everyone, from manager to busboy, would do things the way Curt and I would—the Friendly way, with courtesy and respect.

We also had to consolidate our purchasing and ice cream-making operations, so that one central facility could supply all our stores' needs. We broke ground for a manufacturing plant in West Springfield in 1951. After we grew to 50 stores, we needed something even bigger. In 1960, we built a still larger and more modern plant in Wilbraham, Massachusetts. Inside the front entry today there stands a plaque honoring the two best and most steadfast supporters Curt and I ever had. It reads:

> This building is dedicated to Mr. and Mrs. Herbert P. Blake with warm affection...and in appreciation for their confidence and encouragement...and for the qualities of personal industry and vision they inspired in their sons, the founders of Friendly Ice Cream Corporation.

Between 1935 and 1940, when we opened our second store, we employed fewer than a dozen people altogether. During the summers, when ice cream sales were at their heaviest, one or two part-timers would help one of the brothers during the day; another one or two would help the other brother at night. We worked right alongside our employees, sharing equally in the work, no matter what it was. Whether we knew it or not, we were training by example—the best possible way. Once we had grown too big for that, Curt created a training manual and a standardized 18-to-24 month curriculum. It wasn't enough that our new hires learned the mechanics of their jobs. They had to embrace the Friendly "religion."

Bob Gaudrault, himself a graduate of that training, wrote a history of the company—*Beyond the Mark: Friendly 1935-1985*. In it, he talked about how the training benefitted not just trainees but the whole Friendly institution:

> Companies which believe in their people often are pleasantly surprised to see their interest returned in unusual ways...Friendly had such pleasant experiences...A Friendly deliveryman stopped his familiar tractor-trailer on the turnpike, in a snowstorm, to help a stranded motorist... A Friendly store manager keeps his store open all night to provide food and shelter to stranded citizens caught in a major blizzard.

In his book, Bob described, with characteristic candor, the way our culture bound our managers to us (and vice versa):

> As we became managers of the growing number of stores throughout the late 40's and into the 50's, we also became members of the family. Our opinions were not only sought, they were required. And they were listened to. By this time we had come to know the complementary strengths of the Blakes and had learned to respect their opinions and decisions without fear or suspicion. Pres was particularly stubborn at times and discussions could become very heated. We were expected to disagree when we felt the need to and were never criticized for doing so. Curt was more relaxed and flexible but every bit as firm as Pres when it came to living by the principles. Neither one ever disciplined or criticized any of us publicly. When they felt the need to do this, it was always in private and never in anger. We were never diminished nor made to feel humiliated but we always knew exactly where we stood.

It wasn't enough for us to treat customers with respect. We showed respect for every member of our team. The payoff was a loyalty and commitment that became legendary in the food service industry. It helped ensure the satisfaction of our customers, which laid the foundation for our continued success.

THE BEST ADVICE I EVER SOUGHT

As the pace of Friendly's growth accelerated, we needed advice on lots of things. What different skills would we need to manage 100 stores instead of 50? How could we continue to recruit, and more importantly, to retain the best people? And how could we motivate them to stick with us long-term? I was fortunate to receive invaluable advice from some of the best business leaders in history. How did I get this advice? I asked them.

When Friendly had grown to ten or fifteen stores, I attended a dinner one night where the speaker was the famous retailer J.C. Penney.

He was probably 80 or 85 then, and I must have been about 40. After his speech I approached him to ask if I could visit him to get advice. "Mr. Penney, we're building a business something like yours. You had 2,200 stores, and we're trying to do the same." He said he'd be glad to talk, if I'd just come down to New York.

I remember going to his office, on the top floor of the Penney Building. The man had self-confidence to spare, but no vanity. His office, though paneled beautifully, wasn't opulent by today's standards. When I read today that the John Thains of the world apparently think nothing of lavishing more than a million dollars on their offices, I think back to Mr. Penney. Sadly, I don't remember everything we talked about. But I remember one detail clearly. I asked him the question that mattered to me most: could a businessman be both ethical and prosperous?

His answer was clear and unambiguous: yes. The head of an organization has to be absolutely ethical—and so does every other employee, right on down the line. Dishonesty of any sort cannot be tolerated. Mr. Penney instilled in me the importance of being honest. I've lived by that principle ever since, and I've never hesitated to fire anybody I found stealing or lying or doing anything unethical. It pained me to have to fire some of those people, but out they went. The potential cost of dishonesty was just too high to be tolerated.

Mr. Penney was like a god to me. Many years later, after he died, I took great satisfaction in nominating him for *Fortune's* Business Hall of Fame and attending the banquet celebrating his induction.

Once he and I became friends, I traveled with him. He invited me to his birthday parties and dinners at his home.

Mr. and Mrs. Penney lived at 888 Park Avenue. One night we sat around their library and talked. There was no liquor. Mr. Penney wouldn't have liquor in his house. The maid announced that dinner was ready. We got up to leave the library for the dining room, and, as we left, Mr. Penney waited to be the last one out. As he went by the light switch, he very quietly shut it off. He was always watching expenses, even five cents worth! That made an impression on me. Thrift was in his bones.

As Friendly continued growing, I knew we had to remain vigilant about our ethics. We needed to find the fairest way to compensate executives. I wondered what kind of compensation works best to motivate senior management and keep people honest.

I decided to ask the smartest businessperson in the world. In the 1960s, I figured the smartest businessperson in the world would naturally be the head of the biggest corporation: General Motors. Harlow Curtice had just retired as president of GM. He rescued the Buick brand, restyling it into an object of middle-class desire. He added those four little eye-catching "portholes" on the fenders, which became Buick's signature. Mr. Curtice was *Time's* Man of the Year for 1955, the first businessman given that honor since Walter Chrysler in 1928 (and the last until Ted Turner in 1991).

I wrote to Mr. Curtice, saying that my brother and I had a business and that we would like to discuss with him the best way for us to compensate our managers. "We would greatly treasure a conversation with you," I wrote, "a man who has attained the same high status in your industry as we are striving to do in ours. Please know that we are not looking for money, favors or anything else—just exposure to a man we admire."

I still recall my excitement when I got his letter of response: "If you're ever out this way, I'd be glad to talk with you." Wow! You could bet we'd be out that way, and fast.

I telephoned his office at the Flint National Bank where he was honorary chairman. I assured his secretary we'd take no more than an hour of his time. I prepared eight questions to ask. Curt and I headed out to Michigan.

He was a handsome, distinguished man with reddish hair and a mustache. He was dressed in a tweed suit.

We got right to our eight questions.

During our conversation, Mr. Curtice became very interested in us and what we were trying to do. Our appointment had been for 1:30 pm. At 4:00 pm his secretary dropped in to remind him, "Mr. Curticc, you have an appointment at 4:15."

"Tell them I will be a little late," he said.

We talked about many things that day, including the big bonus Mr. Curtice had earned in his last year at the helm of GM. He'd been paid a salary of $700,000 plus a $200,000 bonus. I wanted to know how important a motivator the bonus had been, since, after taxes, it amounted to relatively little—perhaps $18,000.

The bonus, Mr. Curtice said, had been very important to him.

"Monetarily it didn't do me much good," he explained. "But it was a big boost to my morale. To me it was a confirmation that the Board thought I was doing a good job." After that, we always made sure our best people got good bonuses.

We asked him to explain what he saw to be the relative value of different corporate positions, when it came to compensation. If the president or CEO gets paid X dollars, what percent of X should the treasurer get? How about executive vice president, or the vice president of manufacturing? And so on. Mr. Curtice said he'd put us in touch with a man who could explain it all to us. That man was Tom Murphy, who later became GM's chairman and a dear friend to me.

The immediate result of our meeting with him was that I decided we needed to start giving our managers stock as part of their compensation, as a motivator to help build the company's success by building their own. Curt at first resisted the idea, but eventually he agreed it was a good idea. It was. I think it was just about the smartest thing we ever did because our employees were rewarded when the company did well.

I remained a lifelong friend of Tom Murphy. A few years ago, I wrote him a letter after seeing him in the hospital shortly before his death. I noted, "I think of you so often, because you and I have the same standards of ethics that are very important to both of us."

BIRTH OF THE FRIBBLE

ON FRIENDLY'S MENU, THERE'S A STORY BEHIND practically every item that you see.

Take the Fribble.

"Fribble" is the name for our extra-thick, extra-delicious milkshake. People always want to know how we came up with the name.

Our original milkshake wasn't called the Fribble. It was called something else: the Awful-Awful.

In 1938, when we'd been in business three years, we helped a family in New Jersey get started in the ice cream business. They were like us—a father, a mother, and two sons—and they called their milkshake the "Awful-Awful." That was short for "Awful Big-Awful Good." We liked that, and we asked them if we could use it. They agreed, as a courtesy. We didn't pay them any royalties. They were grateful for our help, so they let us use the name.

We called our milkshakes Awful-Awfuls until we expanded to New Jersey, their home territory. They then told us, very kindly, that they'd prefer to be the only ones in New Jersey using that particular name. We agreed to change the name of ours to something else. But what?

We started a contest among Friendly employees to see who could come up with the best new name. We got lots of suggestions. One of them was "Fribble."

It's a real word. If you look it up in Merriam-Webster's Unabridged Dictionary, you'll see "fribble" defined as a "frivolous thing."

The New Jersey family later went out of business. I guess we could have gone back to using the name Awful-Awful. But we thought Fribble was just better-better!

When it comes to sandwiches, I've always maintained that the best one we ever came up with was the "Big Beef." Hamburgers were our best-selling food item. But we needed some clever way to make them even more appealing.

We made a bigger patty and shaped it in a square, and we served it on bread rather than on a roll. It looked big. It was big. So we dubbed it "Big Beef," and it was an instant hit. The generous hunk of meat looked even bigger sandwiched between thin-sliced bread. All the emphasis was where it should be: on the filling. If you serve a sandwich on a big flouncy bun, you get a big mouthful of bread. With hamburgers, if there's a big glob of bread you can't taste the meat. So the Big Beef doesn't just look big, it delivers a big taste. No wonder customers love it.

Lest you think our menu innovations were all inspired by genius, I can tell you they were not.

We had our duds. High on the list would be the idea of putting vanilla ice cream on cereal.

Never heard of it? There's a reason: It's a bad idea!

In the few Friendly locations where breakfast was served, we tried it. Once. Customers unhesitatingly turned thumbs down, and we discontinued the experiment.

Breakfast itself was a departure for Friendly. Our store managers, for the most part, didn't like the idea of offering it. They believed that the added hours would be too wearing on the staff and would distract attention from our primary daytime business.

WITH HARD WORK YOU GET DESSERT

THROUGHOUT THE 1960S AND 70S, CURT AND I CONTINUED to grow our business by prudent, gradual expansion, reaching heights the two Blake brothers of the 1930s could never have imagined. These were years of tremendous change. Music changed. Women's hemlines went up. And up. And up again. There was the Vietnam War, the war on poverty, the civil rights movement. It's amazing how much Friendly, tossed upon these changing seas, kept to its course and remained fundamentally the same. The formula Curt and I had hit upon by trial and error with our first store—a simple, wholesome menu offered at a fair price and served by a sincerely friendly staff—continued to win customers and keep them coming back.

It's not that we stood still. Hardly. We went public in the stock market in 1968. The stock was initially offered at $28 and hit a high of $52 that same opening day. Paine Webber said they could have sold all 250,000 shares in Springfield, but we wanted to offer the stock nationwide. 25,000 of the shares were sold to managers of Friendly shops.

The sale of stock gave us the resources to expand even more aggressively. In the next decade, Friendly grew from 200 stores to 276, spreading throughout New England and into New York and New Jersey. Later, we expanded into the Midwest, with mixed success.

We remained on the lookout to improve the way we ran things, to improve food quality, and to experiment with new items on the menu. But it's harder to maneuver a battleship than a rowboat, and tinkering with procedure at hundreds of stores is harder than at a single shop you run all by yourself. Friendly, by the late 1970s, was still a friendly place. But it was also a huge, well-oiled machine.

Bob Gaudrault, writing his book in the 1980s, described—rather poetically, I think—how that machine worked:

> Early Monday morning is an interesting time to visit the Friendly plant in Wilbraham. Lights begin to go on as maintenance workers arrive and the early production and distribution shifts begin to fill the parking lots. As the hundreds of food processors and ice cream makers and fork lift operators and shipping clerks move into the buildings, Friendly slowly comes to life; a sleeping giant preparing to reach out to its network of restaurants waiting to receive the hundreds of items needed every day. Diesel engines bark into the morning silence as they push and pull their huge refrigerated trailers up to the loading docks. Forty-five of these sparkling rigs will carry the tons of products to all of the stores. They will travel thousands of miles every day and

> visit Friendly restaurants in 17 states. Later in the morning, other trailer trucks begin arriving at the receiving docks with the products to be stored and processed inside the plant. Entire trailer loads of french fries are frequent visitors each week. A seemingly endless stream of stainless steel tankers filled with milk and cream and sweeteners. Whole trailerloads of soup and clam chowder and tuna fish and mayonnaise. All are quickly and efficiently taken in, stored, and processed, soon to be shipped out again.

We didn't keep our accounts on shirt cardboards any more. We were approaching 600 stores with annual sales of $200 million.

Every day was a new adventure to me during these years, and I never tired of the challenge. If I'd had my way, I'd have kept growing and growing until we had 2,000 restaurants. I was sure I had the drive and the ability to run a company that size. Heck, I was only a young guy in my early sixties!

Curt, however, did not share my gusto. Over the years he and I gradually came to disagree on certain issues that would arise from time to time. Since I was the older brother and tended to hold my views more strongly than Curt, he was more inclined to acquiesce. In order to insure harmony within the top management of the company, Curt decided to step back from his role and retire early.

Curt had the satisfaction of knowing what a vital role he played in the building of a great company. He handled construction, personnel, and training, among other things; I handled purchasing real estate, and finances. He also has been kind enough to acknowledge my contribution to the company, saying, "If it weren't for you, I'd probably be pumping gas today."

However, much of our wealth was tied up in Friendly stock.

Even after our public offering, together we owned 40% of the company.

At Curt's suggestion, we sat down together to consider the sale of the company, and with mixed emotions on both our parts, agreed that the time had come. And so, in 1979, we sold the company to Hershey Foods, who paid $162 million to the shareholders, including Curt and me.

I don't remember if Hershey asked me to stay on. The fact is, I didn't want to stay. Friendly had a very good management team in place by then. Hershey was a great fit for Friendly. As for me, I had other things to do.

People ask if it was a hard transition, going from being the head of a big company one day to being a retiree the next. It wasn't hard at all. I don't remember thinking much about it at the time. One day I was at my desk at Friendly, and the next day—poof!—I wasn't. I don't even think there was a going away party. We just left.

I didn't feel any imperative to spend the money. Some people might have said, "I'll buy a brand new house." But I already had two houses, and I liked them fine. One is the same house I've lived in for 36 years. It's just not my nature to go crazy with money.

How was I going to spend my time?

That, too, wasn't an issue.

There always had been—and there still is—plenty of work to be done on my homes in Florida and Connecticut.

Helen and I love to have family and friends come visit us. Just recently we had a woman who had worked for Friendly for 25 years come and stay. She told her friends she was treated like a queen and never had such a time. It's fun to be nice to people.

I enjoyed having more time to sail my yacht and to travel. I've been around the world eleven times!

During my retirement, I built up my collection of Rolls-Royces to 24. Sometimes, in the evening, I still like to drive one of them after dark, when there's nobody around and it's just the car and me on a quiet country road.

When you have money, you're in a position to help other people, which I've always tried to do.

My hard work at Friendly made a lot of wonderful things possible. This isn't to brag. That's not Pres Blake. I want to give you—especially anyone young who might be reading this—a taste of how much fun you can have if you work hard, look for opportunities, mind your manners, and stay smart. I really believe that if I could do it, so can you.

There's More to Life Than Friendly's

People

HARU

THE MOST REMARKABLE FRIENDSHIP OF MY EARLY LIFE BEGAN when I was 13.

The year was 1927, and Lindbergh had just flown the Atlantic. As an amateur but enthusiastic stamp collector, I was eager to collect Lindbergh stamps. I wrote to the "Mail Bag" column in the *Christian Science Monitor* looking for a pen pal with whom I could correspond and trade stamps.

After a few months, I got a letter from Haru Matsukata in Tokyo, Japan, with some new Japanese stamps. It was a pretty noncommittal letter, but it got our friendship started. I was a fairly good letter writer, and Haru was very good. We kept at it, corresponding once a month.

In one letter, Haru mentioned that the Matsukata family had entertained a famous Christian Science lecturer, John Randall

Dunn, while he was touring Japan. A few months later, Dunn was lecturing in Hartford. I asked my parents if we could go. We did, and, afterwards, I introduced myself to Mr. Dunn.

"I have been writing to a boy in Japan by the name of Haru Matsukata," I said. "What can you tell me about him?"

"About him?" Dunn asked, surprised. "Haru is a girl!"

Well, I was thunderstruck—and humiliated. At 13 years old, it seemed embarrassing to be writing to a girl without realizing it.

I thought back. There had been nothing whatsoever in my pen pal's letters that had given me a clue to the writer's gender. And there had been nothing in my letters, I realized, that had betrayed my ignorance of the fact that he was a she. Still, I felt mortified.

I didn't want her to know I'd been fooled, so I asked her to send me a picture.

When it arrived, I saw not only that Haru was a girl, but that she was a very pretty one. I kept on writing.

We wrote back and forth about all sorts of things, including cars. I remember she liked a 1933 Ford convertible—tan with red wheels. We wrote about our favorite songs. A very popular song at the time was Cole Porter's "Night and Day." We both liked that song.

After a while our letters took on a different tone.

The closings changed from "Affectionately yours," to "With much love." The salutations changed from "Dear Pres" to "Dearest Pres." I guess you could say we fell in love by mail.

I saw Haru in person for the first time in 1933. I met her at the ship when she arrived in New York City on her way to Principia College in St. Louis, Missouri. It was quite a thrill to be confronted for the first time by this lovely girl whom I had come to know so well by mail. She was far prettier than her picture. Her English was excellent, since her family had always retained an English governess.

While she was in the U.S. our friendship blossomed into something more than just correspondence flirtation.

In the summers, I enjoyed taking Haru to fancy places to eat and to dance, because she was such good company. She caused no few eyes to turn her way, because her summer sailing tan contrasted so strikingly with her white sport clothes. Her grandparents lived near Greenwich, Connecticut, and it was always a wonderful experience to spend a weekend there, amidst all the people of Japanese birth, including the servants.

Years later I learned Haru belonged to one of Japan's foremost families. Still later, I found out her paternal grandfather was a prince who had served as prime minister of Japan in the 1920s.

Haru's mother had been responsible for introducing Christian Science to Japan. My own mother, being an ardent Christian Scientist, developed quite a nice rapport with her.

When Haru finished college she returned to Japan. By then she was engaged to an American boy, whom she had met at Principia. We continued to write, albeit more infrequently.

Then the war came and all correspondence stopped. In one of the last letters I received, she wrote about how concerned everyone in Japan was that the militarists were coming to power.

After World War II ended, she wrote again. She described her wartime gardening and her work as a newspaper correspondent.

She had not married, she wrote. But by then I had married Della Deming, so I told her about my wife and my present life. We exchanged pictures again and wrote more, catching each other up on our changing lives.

Haru continued her work as a journalist after the war, even writing articles for the *Saturday Evening Post*. I remember how proudly I read her story of what happened to Japanese aviators after the war.

Eventually, I heard through one of Haru's sisters that Haru was engaged to Edwin Reischauer, a Harvard professor.

Reischauer was American, born of missionary parents in Japan, and spoke fluent Japanese. His wife had died, and he had taken a sabbatical to Japan with his three children. It was in Japan that he met Haru and married her.

I wrote to congratulate her and express my delight that she would be returning to the U.S. to live near Harvard, just 80 miles east of Springfield. She wrote back, saying they would need a car when she got to Massachusetts. Knowing my great love for cars, she asked if I could find her one for a reasonable price. She said they were trying to save money and needed something inexpensive.

We met Haru and Ed at a pier in New York at 8:00 on a Monday morning in August. It was the same pier where I had first met her 25 years earlier.

At first, they borrowed our station wagon, and then I found them a new Ford at a very reasonable price. They didn't want to spend the money on a heater or a radio. But I said, "The heck with that," and paid extra for a radio, a heater, and an automatic transmission.

"You can pay for the car," I told her. "But my wife and I want to pay for the extras. I think you might be the first girl to get an automatic transmission, heater, and radio as a wedding present."

As the months went by, we visited back and forth by phone and by letter. The following summer, Della and I invited them to go sailing with us.

We started with a trip to Provincetown to see a replica of Columbus's ship, the *Santa Maria*, enter Provincetown harbor. We anchored overnight at Plymouth, then made our way from Rhode Island to the Connecticut shore, tying up in Greenwich, close to where Haru's grandfather had once lived. We then sailed up the Hudson River to Albany.

Friendly, by that time, had started opening stores at a rate of two or three a year. We returned from our sailing trip just in time to preside over the opening a big new store in Worcester, Massachusetts, which Curt and I dedicated to our friend and mentor, J.C. Penney.

We organized a big dinner the night before the opening and made quite a big thing of it. We invited Mr. Penney, of course, plus Ed and Haru and all the bankers and senior business leaders of Worcester. I think maybe it was at this dinner that Haru finally had her eyes opened to the fact that Pres Blake—the kid she had written to all those years—had become a pretty prominent and prosperous businessman.

When she got back to Japan, she wrote a story about Friendly titled, "It Can Only Happen in America," which ran on the front page of Tokyo's leading newspaper, the *Asahi Times.*

In 1962, President Kennedy appointed Ed Reischauer ambassador to Japan. Ed was a college professor, not a diplomat. But he fit the bill perfectly, steeped in Japanese culture and married to a Japanese wife who spoke perfect English and Japanese.

Now it was my turn to be impressed by her—to think that my young pen pal was now not only married to America's ambassador to Japan, but living in the same mansion where General Douglas MacArthur had ruled postwar Japan.

SPRINGFIELD TECHNICAL COMMUNITY COLLEGE

In 1963 then Secretary of War, Robert McNamara announced he was closing the Springfield Armory. This was devastating news to the city. The armory had been the backbone of Springfield's economy ever since George Washington chose to build the new nation's armory here.

I sat back and started thinking. I concluded that a man in McNamara's position was not going to change his mind, but the mayor was going to go down to Washington and the senators and representatives were going to try to wring McNamara's arm, and everybody was going to spin their wheels.

So, I wrote a letter to Dick Garvey, editor of the Springfield Daily News, who was a personal friend. I said, you know you aren't going to change this man's mind. Stop running down to Washington. Don't waste your time. Let's aggressively start thinking of what would be the best alternative use for the property, and I had a suggestion.

I pointed out that it was a big campus in the middle of a working class neighborhood and converting those long, brick buildings into college classrooms and dormitories would be a lot easier than trying to make it into a factory. It could be bought from the government for a dollar and using it as a college wasn't going to hurt the taxpayers, because it was already off the tax rolls. I said it ought to be a school or a college. That's all I said.

Now, Garvey went and printed it in Letters to the Editor. This was just a personal letter to him, but he put it in Letters to the Editor. It just so happened that I was leaving for Hong Kong the next day to pick up my new boat, so it hit the paper the day after I left.

All hell broke loose. The union said that dirty, stinking Blake. He's against unions. He's making lousy suggestions. He doesn't care anything about the city of Springfield. The telephone at the plant office was ringing off the hook with people wanting to give that no good Pres Blake, a piece of their mind. And my brother took it on the chin. He had to do the answering for me. And I hadn't discussed my letter with him.

I didn't find out about the ruckus until I got to Hong Kong and talked to Curt on the phone.

Four or five years later after Springfield Technical Community College had become a reality on the armory site I was having dinner with Dick Garvey and told him that he'd die if he ever knew how much trouble that letter had caused me and the company. "Pres, it was that letter of yours that gave us the idea," he said. "It was the best thing that happened and that's why the paper pushed it."

HOPE COOKE

I'VE MET SOME FASCINATING PEOPLE IN MY LIFE WHO HAVE become friends. Hope Cooke is one such person. Today, she lives quietly in the U.K., but at one time, she was featured regularly in *Vogue* and *The New Yorker*, and nicknamed the "Grace Kelly of the Far East."

Hope's parents had already divorced before she was born in 1941. When she was two, her mother died, and she was brought up by her wealthy grandparents and then by her aunt and uncle, a U.S. ambassador to Iran and Peru. She never really felt she had a home. She went to Sarah Lawrence College and became an excellent writer.

While in college, Hope traveled to India and met the crown prince of the kingdom of Sikkim, Palden Thondup Namgyal. Sikkim was a very small mountain kingdom high up in the

Himalayas, between Tibet and India.

In 1963 they were married, and soon afterward he became the king, or chogyal; Hope became the gyalmo (queen).

John Kenneth Galbraith, ambassador to India at the time, attended her wedding, and it was written up in a colorful way for *National Geographic*. She lived in the palace in Gangtok, the capital of Sikkim.

Hope publicly announced she was lonesome and would welcome any Americans who would like to come visit her. I was intrigued. My daughter Nancy and I were planning a trip to the Far East and I suggested we try to meet Hope.

We landed at Tokyo, then went to Hong Kong and on to New Delhi, where we went to Bagdogra Indian Air Force base at the foot of the Himalayas. There we asked how to get to Sikkim. Is there a bus? No bus. Is there a train? No train. How about a helicopter? No, it was reserved exclusively for the queen.

The only way to get there was to hire a jeep and go 100 miles on winding roads. The way was stony and washed out in parts, but we finally arrived in early evening. Mr. Mendez, Hope's assistant, met us in Gangtok. The main street was the bazaar. On one side was the mountain, and on the other, a sheer drop.

For that first night we were to stay in the soldiers' barracks—really just a tent. It got awfully cold at night there, 10,000 feet up, forty miles from Mount Everest. Nancy got up during the night to stir the ashes in the fire, but she stirred up so much smoke we had to move outside, which was even colder. We had a fitful sleep that night.

Next morning Mr. Mendez came to take us to the palace. In our minds, a palace was a big house. But this palace was modest and painted Chinese red. We sat down in the main living room. I talked to Hope about her life. She was about 25 years old then, and very humble and soft-spoken.

ABOVE
Pres Blake at the first Friendly location

RIGHT
Friendly's open layout helped staff give quick service

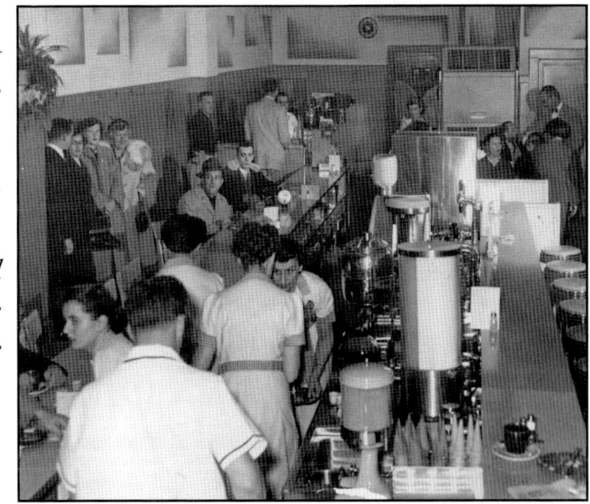

Curtis and Prestley Blake

announce the closing of

Friendly ICE CREAM

Boston Road Store only

this Sunday night, (April 11)

until we win the war!

Our West Springfield store will continue to be open and with no limit on Ice Cream sales.

Friendly Ice Cream suspended operations but didn't close the business during World War II

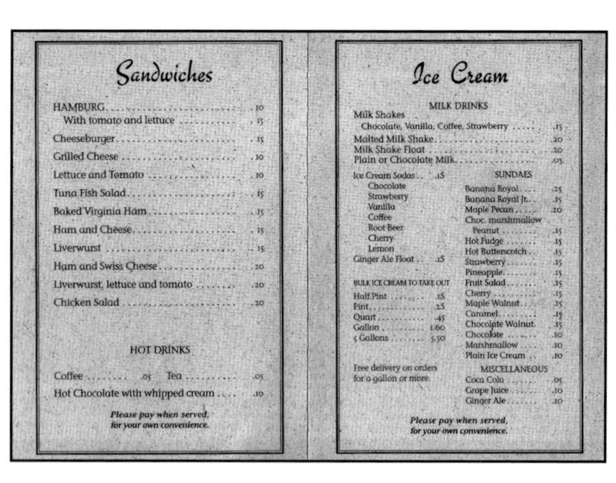

Sandwiches

HAMBURG	.10
With tomato and lettuce	.15
Cheeseburger	.15
Grilled Cheese	.10
Lettuce and Tomato	.10
Tuna Fish Salad	.15
Baked Virginia Ham	.15
Ham and Cheese	.15
Liverwurst	.15
Ham and Swiss Cheese	.20
Liverwurst, lettuce and tomato	.20
Chicken Salad	.20

HOT DRINKS

Coffee	.05
Tea	.05
Hot Chocolate with whipped cream	.10

Please pay when served, for your own convenience.

Ice Cream

MILK DRINKS

Milk Shakes — Chocolate, Vanilla, Coffee, Strawberry	.15
Malted Milk Shake	.20
Milk Shake Float	.20
Plain or Chocolate Milk	.05

Ice Cream Sodas .15
Chocolate
Strawberry
Vanilla
Coffee
Root Beer
Cherry
Lemon

Ginger Ale Float .15

BULK ICE CREAM TO TAKE OUT

Half Pint	.15
Pint	.25
Quart	.45
Gallon	1.60
5 Gallons	5.50

Free delivery on orders for a gallon or more.

SUNDAES

Banana Royal	.25
Banana Royal Jr.	.15
Maple Pecan	.20
Choc. marshmallow Peanut	.15
Hot Fudge	.15
Hot Butterscotch	.15
Strawberry	.15
Pineapple	.15
Fruit Salad	.15
Cherry	.15
Maple Walnut	.15
Caramel	.15
Chocolate Walnut	.15
Chocolate	.10
Marshmallow	.10
Plain Ice Cream	.10

MISCELLANEOUS

Coca Cola	.05
Grape Juice	.10
Ginger Ale	.10

Please pay when served, for your own convenience.

An early Friendly menu—check the prices!

(l to r) Pres Blake and Curt Blake

Ethel and Herbert P. Blake

Pres Blake's first car, a Model T Ford

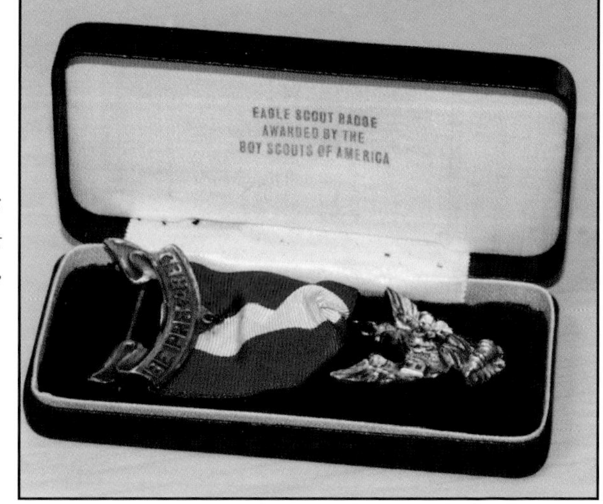

Pres Blake's Eagle Scout Badge

ABOVE

Massachusetts Turnpike, before

BELOW

Same spot on turnpike, after

Pres Blake conceived the idea for this sign. Challenged by the state in court, Pres won the right to keep this display on the side of the road

PHOTO BY JOHN KARAM

Sales by month of Boston Road.

	1936	1937	1938	1939	1940
Jan	486.69	1101.93	1198.18	1660.36	1940.75
Feb	498.51	1015.67	1154.57	1507.02	2115.86
Mar	807.07	1206.37	1604.94	1913.23	2485.12
Apr.	815.47	1525.73	1868.07 ~~1737.92~~	2307.21	2893.32
May	1276.–	2163.51	2177.26	3350.11	3763.92
June	1365.33	2141.05	2402.95	3386.15	4154.33
July	1709.65	2587.85	2873.38	4078.24	5100.66
Aug.	1694.25	2743.64	2956.17	4108.84	4241.66
Sept	1230.45	1866.87	2040.92	3144.19	3595.10
Oct.	1001.64	1529.94	2182.06	2602.08	3033.–
Nov	856.50	1323.91	1841.10	2302.–	2691.11
Dec	962.07	1261.22	1648.46	2059.62	2536.75
1st 6mo	5249.07	9154.26	10405.97 ~~[illegible]~~	14124.08	17353.30
2nd 6mo	7454.56	11,313.43	13,542.09	18295.–	21198.28
Total	12,703.63	20,467.69	23,948.06 ~~[illegible]~~	32419.05	38551.58
10 numb	2673	4517	5389	7414	8237
[illegible]	9011	11,125	13,115	18320	24988

Early sales recorded by Ethel Blake on shirt cardboards

ABOVE

(l to r) McDonald's CEO Ray Kroc and Pres Blake

RIGHT

(l to r) J.C. Penney and Pres Blake

DeWitt Wallace (third from right), founder of Readers' Digest, *with Pres Blake (r) and the Board of Trustees of Northfield Mount Hermon school*

GM chairman Harlow Curtice, Time *magazine's 1955* Man of the Year

ABOVE

Helen and Pres Blake's wedding day in Nantucket

LEFT

Haru Matsukata, a lifelong friend

(l to r) Pres Blake, Exy Johnson, and Captain Irving Johnson

(l to r) Curt Blake, GM chairman Thomas Murphy, and Pres Blake

Sharlene Wells Hawkes (second from right) and her family with Helen and Pres Blake

(l to r) Helen Blake, Hope Cooke, and Pres Blake

LEFT
Pres Blake's yacht America

RIGHT
(l to r) President Jawara of The Gambia and Pres Blake

LEFT
Bell presented as trophy to Pres Blake for first place in yachting race with America

LEFT
Women of The Gambia

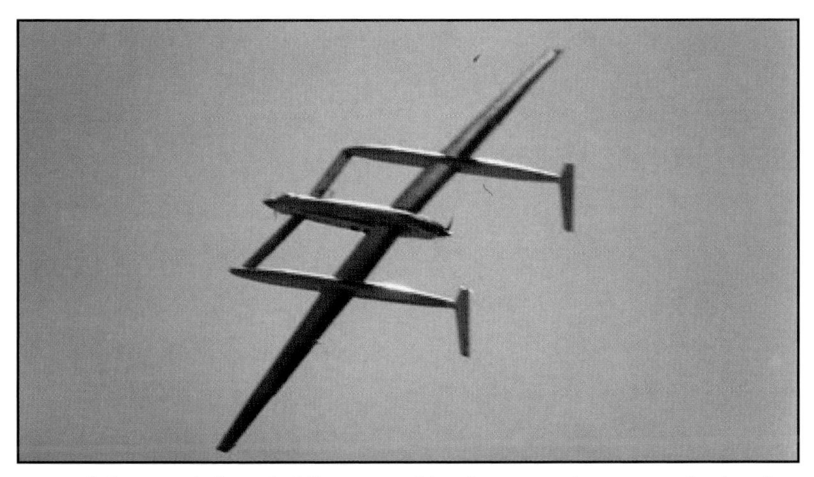

Pres Blake traveled to California and back in two days to see the landing of the Voyager, *the first non-stop airplane trip around the world*

Pres Blake at the North Pole

(l to r) Senator Edward Brooke, Helen Blake, Anne Brooke, and Pres Blake on their Concorde around-the-world trip

Rolls-Royces in front of Pres Blake's Connecticut home

Clenet Coachworks car

Stuart, Florida home of Pres and Helen Blake

(l to r) Lucy Copp, J.C. Penney's great-granddaughter, and Iraq war hero Jessica Lynch, in front of a replica of an Egyptian pyramid built on the grounds of the Blakes' Connecticut home

Tania Aebi (second from left) and her family

(l to r) Jim Weber of Harvard, attorney Jim Donnelly, Prof. Fabrizio Ferri, Pres Blake, Prof. Jay Lorsch, Adam Blake, and Ben Blake, at Harvard Business School's first presentation of its case study Blake v. Friendly Ice Cream Corp.

Helen Blake and Pres Blake as Pres receives honorary degree

Blake Library in Stuart, Florida

ABOVE

(l to r) Helen Blake and Arantxa Castillo

RIGHT

Author Anne Morrow Lindbergh at her 94th birthday in 2000

Blake Student Commons at Bay Path College in Longmeadow, Massachusetts

Blake Arena at Springfield College in Springfield, Massachusetts

Blake Middle School at Wilbraham and Monson Academy in Wilbraham, Massachusetts

S. Prestley Blake Law Center, home to the Western New England College School of Law in Springfield, Massachusetts

Blake Hall at Northfield Mount Hermon School in Mount Hermon, Massachusetts

Springfield Technical Community College in Springfield, Massachusetts—Pres Blake encouraged its establishment at the site of an abandoned World War II armory

1959

2011

Blake Helicopter

Twin Otter at North Pole

Before we left, Hope told us she had been instrumental in building a new library, but that it lacked books. When I got back home I contacted several publishers and secured the end runs of many books. I sent cartons of books to the library. She really appreciated the gesture and never forgot it.

The rest of Hope's story isn't so pretty.

Hope wrote a memoir, *Time Change*, in which she described some difficult times. The king, who was 17 years older than Hope, was a heavy drinker and didn't want to give up his relationships with former girlfriends. Hope was forced to leave Sikkim in 1973 when the political situation in the kingdom became dangerous. In 1975, the king was deposed. Sikkim is now a protectorate of India. Hope returned to New York with her children, was divorced from the king, and later married a professor. Today she is divorced.

In New York, she became an urban historian and wrote a book about city history walks, as well a book with dancer Jacques D'Amboise. She's writing a new book now.

WIVES

Helen

IT'S EASY TO SAY WHAT WAS THE BEST THING I DID IN MY retirement: I got married.

My marriage to Helen Davis wasn't my first. Nor was it hers. But it has been happy from the start. I love to sit across the table and look at her. She's a gorgeous gal. Everybody loves Helen. At night, it makes me happy to reach over and touch her, just to know she's there. I'm not sure why my marriage to Helen has worked out so well and my first two marriages did not. Love is a complicated thing.

I'd known Helen for many years before we married. She was the wife of Jack Davis, a Friendly executive. Together they'd raised four wonderful kids: Paul, Karen, Mark, and Susan. Jack became ill with cancer and died. At Jack's funeral, I stood eight feet behind

Helen as she watched her husband's casket go into the ground, never dreaming I'd someday be married to her. Susan now lives next door to us in Connecticut. Sons Paul and Mark live in Florida and Massachusetts, respectively. Unfortunately, daughter Karen succumbed to cancer in 2005, but we still have her wonderful husband and two lovely daughters.

I dated Helen and we fell in love. But I was reluctant to get married again. I was 17 years Helen's senior. After a poor record of two unsuccessful marriages, I wasn't eager to risk spoiling the last half of her life. But Helen wanted me to marry her, and I was smart enough to see that if I didn't, I might lose this marvelous woman.

Maybe the reason we've been so happy is that we got off to such a good start.

We decided to get married on Nantucket Island. We flew there in my helicopter. It was November 16, 1982—a cool, beautiful, clear day. We skimmed over the sea in the early morning sun. An hour later, we were looking down on the white houses of Nantucket, bright in the sun. We landed and asked a fisherman to take a picture of us standing on the dock. We had lunch and then met the minister.

We walked up to the church on the hill and had our ceremony in the old vestry. The only other people present were Helen's daughter Susan and my son Ben. Our trip home was in the helicopter, which landed back on our own front yard. The whole adventure had taken just six hours. Helen got on the telephone and called my mother. "Mrs. Blake," said Helen, "this is Mrs. Blake!" My mother and Helen were real pals.

Della

MY FIRST WIFE, DELLA DEMING, WAS 22 WHEN WE GOT married, and I was 26. We had two children: our daughter

Nancy Yanakakis, who lives in Coral Gables, and our son Benson (Ben) of Stonington, Connecticut. Ben now has three sons of his own, and Nancy has two girls.

Della, who passed away in 2005, was a very good wife. But over time we grew apart and couldn't get along. After 25 years of marriage, we were divorced.

Setsu

MY SECOND MARRIAGE WAS TO A JAPANESE WOMAN, SETSU Matsukata, the sister-in-law of my pen pal from childhood, Haru. We divorced within five years, but her son Naotaka remained with me to be educated and has matured into a fine man. Our divorce was not bitter as she lived with me, off and on, for five years after the divorce—a rather odd situation.

SADIE HAWKINS

IF YOU LOOK UP "SADIE HAWKINS" ON THE INTERNET, YOU'LL find plenty of question-and-answer sites that say Sadie Hawkins was not a real person—just a fictional character created by cartoonist Al Capp for his "Li'l Abner" comic strip.

But that's not true. Sadie Hawkins was most definitely a real person. How do I know? She was married to my grandfather.

It's a sad story, but a fascinating one.

Sadie Hawkins married my grandfather, Theodore Stewart, in Silver Creek, New York, September 10, 1868. She was a beautiful young woman, by all accounts. After several years, Sadie began having bouts of depression, and sought treatment from Dr. Egerton R. Howie.

Although each of them was married, Sadie and Howie fell in love. Their affair went on for several years and was common knowledge around town. Eventually Sadie went to Buffalo to stay with her brother Mark.

On July 7, 1881, Sadie and Howie registered at a hotel in Niagara Falls under assumed names. They each left letters for their spouses at the hotel, and then, hand in hand, walked toward the American falls. That was the last they were seen.

Their bodies were discovered days later below the falls. The letters they wrote were suicide notes, asking their spouses for forgiveness.

The New York Times published an article July 13, 1881 about Sadie's brother identifying the body. Another article appeared in the *Times* about the letters the couple had left behind that proved their suicide intent. There was a small flurry of public interest in this tragic story.

More than 50 years later, in 1937, Al Capp published a "Li'l Abner" comic strip that included a new character named "Sadie Hawkins." Sadie was a desperate spinster whose father organized a footrace for her to catch a husband. The idea caught on, and "Sadie Hawkins Day" became an unofficial annual holiday, with women using the day to turn the tables on men, asking them to dance or go on a date.

Some people have thought that because Sadie's jump over Niagara Falls received some publicity, Al Capp might have been intrigued by the story and decided to use her name to represent the character he created—a woman who has lost all hope with men. However it happened, he immortalized the name of Sadie Hawkins, doomed wife of my grandfather, Theodore Stewart.

CAPTAIN IRVING JOHNSON

IRVING JOHNSON WAS A HERO IN MY EYES LONG BEFORE I MET him. A professional sailor, Johnson crewed on the tall ship *Peking* in 1929 and made a name for himself sailing treacherous routes around the word. He and his wife Electa, known to everyone as "Exy," sailed seven times around the world, in each trip training a new crew for the rigors of sailing. His first around-the-world ship was a schooner called the *Yankee*, and the second was a Brigantine, also called the *Yankee*.

On each of Johnson's seven trips around the world he left Gloucester, Massachusetts on a specified day and time and returned to Gloucester exactly 18 months later. On the day of return, at exactly 2:00 pm, Johnson would throw the first line ashore. It was quite a show, with banners welcoming the Johnsons and their crew, a band playing, and planes zooming overhead at exactly the right moment. Many of their trips were documented by the *National*

Geographic, as well as in books written by Exy. Their ports of call on these trips were the most exotic places.

During World War II, Johnson joined the U.S. Navy and advised the Pacific Fleet about dangerous areas in the South Seas, based on knowledge about those islands and atolls from his many voyages. Years later, Exy gave Helen a cane brought back from Pitcairn Island in the South Pacific from one of the Johnsons' circumnavigations.

Johnson's last *Yankee* was a ketch. We spent most of our time with Irving and Exy on this ship, sailing the Mediterranean Sea and the rivers in Europe.

Our first trip with the Johnsons was five weeks aboard the *Yankee*, starting at the Greek island of Rhodes in the South Aegean Sea. We visited many islands full of ruins of early Greek life and quaint, colorful architecture. These smaller islands are seldom seen by cruise ships and are best enjoyed by small yachts.

Another voyage took us to Sardinia and Corsica, Napoleon's birthplace, and ended in Marseilles. During that trip, I contracted a case of jaundice. Irving remarked that I must be really sick when I showed no interest in the bikini-clad French girl sunning on the boat next to us at the dock! I went straight home to the hospital.

Della, Nancy, Ben, and I took another sailing trip with the Johnsons to Trondheim, Norway. A 1934 Rolls-Royce with a shiny new body had been delivered at exactly the time of our arrival. We toured in that car—soon covered in Norwegian mud—to Oslo, where we had a brief meeting with King Olav V in his office.

I had marvelous adventures with Irving—a great sailor and friend.

TANIA AEBI

I'VE HAD MY SHARE OF SAILING ADVENTURES, SO NATURALLY, I've always been fascinated by people who make a name for themselves sailing. Tania Aebi is one such sailor.

At seventeen years old, her father gave her a choice. He would pay for college, or buy her a boat. There was one catch: if she chose the boat, she'd have to sail it around the world—alone. She had spent ten months aboard a boat before and sailed across the Atlantic with her family, so she was already an experienced sailor. But solo circumnavigation? She took the challenge.

She sailed from New York harbor in May 1985 to begin a 27,000-mile journey aboard her 26-foot sloop. With only her cat for company, she spent two and one-half years sailing around the world, stopping in 23 countries. At the time, she was the youngest person to sail around the world alone, and remained the youngest woman to do so until 2010. She wrote a fascinating book about her travels, *Maiden Voyage*, which I received as a gift from a friend. I read the book and knew I had to meet this amazing young woman who had the physical and inner strength to finish what she had started.

She visited us in both Florida and Connecticut, and we arranged for her to speak about her voyage to a spellbound audience in Florida. We have visited Tania in Vermont at her lovely home at the edge of a meadow. Her ex-husband Olivier lives just up the road and they raise their two sons together. A few years ago, the couple took turns sailing in the Caribbean and the South Seas with the boys for a year, six months with each parent. Tania wants to be sure her children learn the same love for sailing and for adventure that her father planted in her as a teenager.

SHARLENE WELLS HAWKES

IN THE EARLY 1990S, ESPN2 PRODUCED A SERIES OF SAILING films with introductory pieces hosted by Gary Jobson, a world class yachtsman and television commentator, along with Sharlene Wells Hawkes, an ESPN commentator who had been Miss America 1985. Our neighbor Buzz McCormick suggested that our property at Sailfish Point in Florida would be the perfect venue for the short films. We agreed to the shoot—it sounded like a fun adventure!

The cast and crew were booked in a nearby hotel, but we offered to house Sharlene and Gary so we could get to know them. This began a long standing friendship with Sharlene and her family.

We watched the filming every day. Helen even hung a sign on the back of my chair that said "Director."

Before they arrived, the production company asked if we knew where they could get a high-cut wet suit for Sharlene. In the film,

Sharlene would be flipped into the water out of a small sailboat, and I guess they were looking for a little sex appeal from the former Miss America. When Sharlene arrived she checked out the wet suit. "Oh no," she said in a very sweet voice. Sharlene is a Mormon, married in the Temple, and that wet suit would not do for her. Back it went, and a standard wet suit arrived.

Sharlene is a woman of deep conviction. She showed it several times during the shoot. One film was set in the cockpit of our sailboat. Gary was dressed in a traditional yachting jacket and Sharlene carried a parasol, as if ready to watch the America's Cup races. A waiter carried a silver tray and delivered champagne to them. When Sharlene saw the champagne, she said, "Oh, no. That's alcohol." The property people went running back into the house and asked Helen if they could use our best teacups. When the tea arrived, Sharlene said, "Oh, no. Someone may think it's stimulant tea." Back to the house. The tray arrived again, with fancy flutes of orange juice. I was afraid Sharlene would think they might be mistaken for mimosas, but this time, she gave her okay and the filming went on.

The next time Sharlene came to Florida she was accompanied by Bob, her wonderful husband. The whole Hawkes family, with their four great kids, has become a part of our family, and we have traveled together many times. We have a scrapbook of photos taken on our vacations together at the Grand Canyon, skiing in Utah, at our homes in Florida and Connecticut. Sharlene's dad got us tickets one Christmas to hear the Mormon Tabernacle Choir in concert.

Recently, Sharlene and Bob bought one of my many Thunderbirds. All of the Hawkes fell in love with the car when they were visiting in Connecticut. How could I resist letting them have one (at a very attractive price)?

Places

TO THE GAMBIA...BY YACHT

SOME OF THE GREATEST TRIPS OF MY LIFE HAVE COME ABOUT from my love of sailing.

In 1972 I bought a 105-foot gaff-rigged schooner called *America.* That yacht was a reproduction of a schooner of the same name that in 1851 defeated its British racing competitors so decisively that the America's Cup trophy was named in her honor.

I entered *America* in the Tall Ships race from Copenhagen, Denmark to Gdynia, Poland in 1974. We came in first place in our class, which included 46 square-rigged ships from all over the world.

After the race, we determined that the best route back to the U.S. was south to Africa to catch the trade winds across the south Atlantic. The president of The Gambia, Sir Dawda Jawara, heard of our triumph in the race and our sailing route, and he invited us to visit his country. President Jawara was a sailor, and he was thrilled to have a yacht with the historical significance of *America* visit his small country.

This was a true adventure. In 1974, very few Americans had visited The Gambia. And it was very rare for a boat our size to sail into the heart of The Gambia.

A little geography first. At the westernmost tip of Africa is Dakar, Senegal, and just south of that is the country known as The Gambia. The harbor of the capital city, Banjul, is 2-1/2 miles wide. From there, the Gambia River splits the country, which is only ten miles wide, into two sections. The Gambia River continues all the way into the interior of Africa, about 250 miles, 180 miles of which were navigable by our large yacht.

Writer Mark Gibbons, who was aboard the *America* for its foray into The Gambia, wrote about the trip for *Yachting* magazine. He describes the importance of the Gambia River for the country:

> It is the lifeline of the country, and traffic is heavy its entire length, from single-oared canoes carved from mahogany logs to crudely-built 100-foot sailing barges. Sails of every shape and material are used, with burlap sacks sewn together especially in vogue. Grain, peanuts, lumber, hides, vegetables and fruits make up the cargos, with people and animals jammed in too.

After a ceremonial welcome, President Jawara took the helm of *America* for a test sail. The next day we set out into the heart of The Gambia.

Mark Gibbons describes the scene as *America* headed slowly upriver:

> ...The river narrowed and seemed more exciting and mysterious, its pale, yellow-green surface lined with mangroves for a dozen yards inland, where fields of tall wild grass, the

color of khaki and clotted with leafless, elephant-skin trees, were a setting for herds of wild antelopes and gazelles...egrets, pelicans, buzzards, herons, even eagles, all around us, and strange squawks and cries echoing from the brush.

We weren't in Massachusetts anymore.

The Gambia was a very poor country in the mid-1970s, with an unemployment rate of 70 percent. The main crop of the country was peanuts.

We were as much an exotic sight to the native Gambians as they were to us. When we made our first stop on the Gambia River at the village of Albreda, more than 200 villagers came down to greet us, in native dress of almost every color and description. The villagers lived in small thatched roof mud huts, with as many as twelve family members living in one room. We saw a 20-foot high mound of peanuts, where natives were spent the day sorting out the good nuts from the bad.

There are connections across the Gambia River in only a few places. At one spot on the river, a massive ferry makes a very slow passage between the two banks of the river, with a cargo of everything from goats to mail to people.

Near the village of Kuntaur, some of our party left the yacht to explore the side creeks, which we were told were populated by crocodiles and hippopotamuses. We spotted both types of creatures.

That night, a tribal chief invited us to a tom-tom, a native dance. I've always liked a good dance, so we anchored and off we went.

It was very hot and there was no rain. You could hear the tom-toms beating in the distance. The only light came from torches burning along the dusty path. Soon we reached an open area, where there was a big fire going. There were logs to sit on, and the band was beating the drums.

We sat on the logs around the bonfire and watched by firelight as people danced all kinds of dances, with the tom-toms playing a very unusual beat—I never heard any American drummer play anything like this beat.

After about an hour a young girl came over to me, took me by the hand and indicated she would like to dance with me. I remember her very clearly—a girl, maybe 15 or 16, wearing a long electric-blue dress that went right to the ground. I took her by the hand and said to myself, "Boy, will I ever give you a dance!"

We danced the wildest dance ever. I danced my fool head off.

Everybody cheered. I started crazy-dancing, jumping all around. The girl was doing the same thing. The band played faster and faster. Suddenly I thought to myself, "I'm going to have a heart attack."

Finally the bandleader saw that I was an older, gray-haired guy, and he slowed down. Everybody clapped, and I went back to my seat and just collapsed.

When we got to Banjul, the king gave us a reception. All the ambassadors and their colorfully clad wives were there. They all spoke English. I gave a short speech about how we were trying to sow seeds of peace—the usual stuff people say.

Even though The Gambia was an underdeveloped country, President Jawara was quite sophisticated. He was educated in England and Scotland, and had made several trips to the United States. We were fascinated by the fact that he had two wives: a black wife, who lived in Africa, and a white wife, who lived in London. It was an unusual arrangement.

Before we left The Gambia, I had an idea. I said, "Sir Dawda, I am building a stone house back in Connecticut. Might I take back with me some stones native to your country?" The next morning he sent a whole raft of stones—some big, some small—down to the boat. We took them all aboard, but it was far more than we could carry on the ship for the long voyage back to the United States. I waited until we got out to sea and then threw all but a few away, which I took back home. Those stones are in my house today, with a plaque that reads, "Pudding Stones from The Gambia."

AROUND THE WORLD BY CONCORDE

IN 1999, HELEN AND I—TWO PEOPLE MARRIED BY helicopter—decided we should perpetuate our aviation romance by making a trip around the world on board the Concorde.

The Concorde was the fastest civilian airliner ever built. Today there's nothing like it. Most commercial jets fly at about 575 miles an hour. The Concorde, with a top speed of 1,350, flew faster than the speed of sound. It flew so high—60,000 feet, or 11 miles up—that when you looked out the window, you could see the curvature of the Earth, as if you were in space. The experience was like flying in a spaceship—one with gourmet meals and flight attendants. Only twenty Concordes were ever made, built by the British and the French.

The cabin was luxurious, but it wasn't roomy. It was narrow, and the ceiling was so low, if you were tall, you bumped your head when you stood up. Nor could the Concorde carry many people.

On our flight, there was room for just Helen and me, 94 other lucky adventurers, and the crew.

The 24-day itinerary called for us to depart New York, then make stops in Hawaii, Tahiti, New Zealand, Sydney, Beijing, Hong Kong, New Delhi, Agra, Mumbai, Nairobi, Cairo, Paris, and return to New York. Along the way, we'd stay at the best hotels, visit the world's great cities, and see some of the most beautiful and exotic sights.

An extra pleasure for us was having my friend of many years, Senator Edward Brooke of Massachusetts, and his wife Anne traveling on the same trip. My friendship with him dated back years, to Ed's investment in Friendly stock, which had made him a good profit.

In Hawaii, Helen first balked at the chance to go sightseeing by helicopter. Although she'd flown to and from her own wedding in a helicopter, she'd seen two crashes since then, both involving our own helicopter on our property in Connecticut. But it was the only vantage point from which to see something rare, dramatic, and amazing: red hot lava flowing from the lip of a volcano downward to the sea, where contact with the cold water sent clouds of white steam skyward.

In New Zealand, we bounced around in high-speed jet boats on the Shotover River—an experience that left our hearts racing and our bodies eager to get back onto dry land.

Elsewhere in New Zealand, near Arrowhead, we watched open-mouthed as young people bungee jumped from a high bridge spanning a deep gorge. It was frightening just to watch: the divers, an elastic cord tied around their legs, threw themselves into space hoping that the cord would stop them just in time from dashing out their brains against the rocks some 140 feet below. A number of watchers were so unnerved that they had to walk away. Not Ed Brooke.

Ed, who at that time was just about to celebrate his 80th

birthday, somehow got it into his head that he wanted to jump. He was nearing the front of the line of would-be jumpers when Anne rushed over. Ed recounted the moment in his 2006 memoir, *Bridging the Divide*. Anne, who never raised her voice, pushed through the crowd, screaming, "What are you doing?" She stopped Ed from bungee jumping, which I think he's always regretted—a little.

Our next stop was China, where we arrived at a very special time: the 50th anniversary of the founding of the People's Republic of China. Because the Concorde created a sonic boom wherever it went, the Chinese government was concerned the loud noise might alarm the people of Beijing. Instead, we were instructed to land at Tianjin, a two-hour drive from Beijing. We were told that immigration officials would be strict and would process us one by one, that we could expect delays, and that we should keep to our seats and follow their instructions to the letter.

These warnings left us a little apprehensive about what kind of reception we could expect once we left the Concorde. The greeting, much to our relief, was the warmest of any we received on the entire trip. As we walked down the Concorde's stairway, a red carpet was spread before us and music was being played in our honor by 100 young people dressed in red and white uniforms. Two hours later, after a ride over bumpy roads, we arrived at Beijing's Shangri La Hotel, whose staff gave us a second warm and hospitable welcome.

The next day we toured the city, now bustling with preparations for the celebration of the 50th anniversary of the Republic's founding. Our guides, who were extremely knowledgeable and spoke perfect English, surprised us by confiding that they thought some of the government's rules were "significant mistakes." One shared a Chinese adage with us: "A lucky man has an American salary, a British house, Chinese food and a Japanese wife. An unlucky man has a Chinese salary, a Japanese house, British food and an American wife." Some of us thought it was funny!

We climbed the Great Wall. Hardly less vast, it seemed to us, was Tiananmen Square, bedecked for the upcoming anniversary with bright lights and huge posters of Chairman Mao. The square, surrounded by government buildings, was packed with tourists, students in bright yellow jackets, families, children, and soldiers, most of them unarmed young boys. Though the atmosphere was festive, I could not help but remember the uprising that had taken place here ten years earlier, in which many brave young anti-government protesters had died.

On the morning of September 27, as we prepared to leave Beijing, the entire staff of the Shangri La assembled curbside to wave us their goodbyes—one last expression of China's incomparable hospitality.

Later that day we landed in Hong Kong, at what was then a brand new airport, chiseled out of sheer rock on the west side of the island. Construction of it turned out to be far more expensive than had been estimated—Hong Kong's version of Boston's over-budget "Big Dig."

I had visited Hong Kong many times before. Along with Cape Town, South Africa, it is one of my two favorite cities in the world, with their beautiful harbors surrounded by sea and mountains. The famous Peninsula Hotel, where Helen and I stayed, had a fleet of Rolls-Royces to take guests to and from the airport and on tours sponsored by the hotel. I visited the garage where they stored all twelve of them.

From our room, we enjoyed a magnificent view of the harbor. I recalled my visit to Hong Kong years before to take delivery of a sailboat. What a thrilling adventure that was, sailing late at night into the Hong Kong harbor, careful not to hit the big, unlighted mooring buoys used by freighters awaiting dock space in the teeming port.

Although shopping is the big thing to do in Hong Kong, Helen and I restrained ourselves, knowing that anything we bought would have to be shipped home. Cargo space onboard the Concorde was severely limited.

We flew next to India, landing in New Delhi, then to Agra, home of the fabled Taj Mahal, justly considered one of the Seven Wonders of the World. My first trip here had been with my daughter Nancy on our way to Sikkim, high in the Himalayas. On that trip I saw the Taj Mahal at night, its silvery dome bathed in the light of a full moon, a sight I will never forget. On this trip, India's poverty—no less forgettable—awed Helen and me. But we left full of hope that India, which already has achieved so much economic progress, will find a way to lift the living standards of its people.

In Africa, our next stop, we stayed at the Masai Mara Reserve in Kenya in a tented camp called Kichwa Tembo. Our first morning there, we arose before dawn to join other guests for a hot air balloon flight over the African grasslands. Floating 200 feet above the ground, we watched herds of antelopes, lions, gazelles, zebras, giraffes, and elephants feeding on the dusty plains. As the bright sun rose, it cast dramatic shadows over a magical landscape. We saw hippopotamuses, rhinos, and grazing herds of deceptively docile water buffalo. When our balloon touched down, the basket unceremoniously tipped over on its side. We scrambled out to find a champagne breakfast waiting for us. That night we watched the sun set over the Oloololo Escarpment as we warmed ourselves by a huge bonfire and enjoyed fine native cuisine on the banks of the Mara River.

Our trip ended in Paris, where we stayed two days at the Hotel de Crillon before returning to our home in Stuart, Florida.

We came away from the experience very much impressed by the Concorde's captain Jacques Chauvin and his crew, who, in the course of our circumnavigation, had executed 28 flawless takeoffs and landings. It was with much regret that we learned a few months later of the death of one fine young member of our crew, killed along with 112 other people when a Concorde leaving Paris crashed on takeoff after hitting debris on the runway. This tragic accident effectively ended the Concorde's career. The surviving planes were either mothballed or donated to aircraft museums around the world—a sad end to a magnificent means of transportation. We were lucky to have made this trip when we did.

THE NORTH POLE—TWO WAYS

I'VE BEEN AROUND THE WORLD ELEVEN TIMES AND OVERSEAS over 80 times. When I heard about a trip to the North Pole, I signed up right away! There are only about six weeks a year when the trip can be made, when the snow and ice conditions are suitable. I brought my son Ben and his new wife Teresa with me. We met in Edmonton, Alberta and took local planes to Yellow Knife and to Cornwallis Island, the last stop before the North Pole.

Before landing at the North Pole, our Twin Otter plane was filled with drums of fuel and was equipped with skis and wheels that dropped down through openings to be used when needed. If the snow is hard-packed, the pilots use the wheels and in soft snow they raise the wheels and use skis. In the ten minutes it took us to circle the North Pole looking for a place to land, we passed through all 24 time zones!

Near the North Pole, we built an igloo where we spent the

night, clothed but comfortable. I hoisted the flag of my yacht at the North Pole.

Pan Am hosted a trip around the world in the 1970s to show the long-range capabilities of their 747SP ("SP" stands for "special performance"). In 42 hours we flew from New York to Delhi, on to Tokyo and back to New York. I suggested that Pan Am consider having a trip to both the North and South Poles. About a year and a half later, in October 1977, they scheduled such a trip, and I signed on with gusto, and invited Ben and Teresa.

There were about 100 passengers, including some fashion models to make the flight more glamorous. We went from San Francisco over the North Pole, and the models put on a show of furs as we flew over the Pole. Then we landed in London, to stop and pick up Miss U.K. Next stop was the South Pole. As we passed over the pole, two of the models kissed me, one on each cheek. Now that's the way to travel.

Things

ROLLS-ROYCE

RETIREMENT ALLOWED ME TO DEEPEN MY LOVE AFFAIR WITH beautiful automobiles—Rolls-Royces in particular—which had started in my boyhood, back in Springfield, the only place outside England where Rolls-Royces have ever been built.

There's something about the beauty of their construction that I find satisfying: the care and finesse, the attention to detail down to the smallest parts. I admire the engines, the leather, the fine matched veneers used in the coach work. I appreciate these machines the way somebody else appreciates a fine work of art.

I still own the first one I ever bought.

The year was 1955, and it was a 1925 Rolls-Royce chassis. It belonged to a college professor at Springfield College who had bought it used for $100 and lovingly restored it. It was the most fantastic mechanical re-creation—it ran silently, perfectly, like a top. I paid $2,000.

I didn't want to drive it as just a chassis, so I started looking for a body. Eventually I found one that was being stored in a barn on a farm in Purchase, New York. I bought it for $700. On December 31, 1955, I headed to Purchase, driving the open chassis—just me, a bucket seat, and a windshield. Oh, it was cold! Freezing! I had on a pile of jackets and I wore a face mask with nothing but slits for my eyes and my mouth, but still, I was cold.

I remember going through a toll booth on the Connecticut Turnpike. Picture it: an old Rolls-Royce with no body on it coming down the road on New Year's Eve, driven by a character in a full face mask. When I reached up to hand the toll taker my money, he turned to his colleague and said, "Now I've seen everything."

When I got to the farm, I took the body stored in the barn and mated it to my chassis. The ride home was warmer, I can tell you!

That car was beautiful, but it took work. I had it painted. I had new leather put in, a new top added. When it was perfect, I took it to a 1957 Rolls-Royce owners' meet, and it won first prize.

Over the years I bought more Rolls-Royces and enjoyed tinkering with them and modifying them. I've always loved touring cars, so I had a new four-passenger Rolls-Royce touring car—no windows, no side curtains—made from a sedan. All the lumber came from trees on our property in Connecticut. The windowsills are black walnut, and the wooden top bows and the nailing strip are ash.

My collection, at its biggest, consisted of 24 of these fantastic cars. To house them all, I had a big barn built at my home in Connecticut. Today I still own five.

These cars have brought me all kinds of pleasure. They're a joy to drive. It's been fun to go to Rolls-Royce meets and take trips with other owners. I've made some good friends that way.

One unexpected bonus of my hobby came in 1969.

Otto Preminger, the film director, was making a movie starring Liza Minelli, *Tell Me That You Love Me, Junie Moon*. The producers wanted a blue Rolls-Royce for the film. Their scout went looking in Boston and couldn't find one. A car dealer there told them about my collection.

The scout came to visit and I showed him my cars. I thought he would pick my blue Rolls-Royce convertible. But he saw my blue Silver Ghost and wanted that one. It was very complicated to drive, so they asked if I would be willing to play the chauffeur in the movie and drive the car. I did it. There's a scene with me and my car in the movie. There's also a scene where Liza Minelli, in silhouette, strips by moonlight in a cemetery. That's probably more compelling than me and my car!

CLENET COACHWORKS

My interest in beautiful cars led me to a short business venture with a car company. Just after my "retirement" in 1979, my friend Briggs Cunningham told me about a man who was building sports roadsters in Santa Barbara, California. The man's name was Alan Clenet, and he built a fine car made entirely from off-the-shelf parts, starting with a Lincoln chassis and a Ford motor.

Clenet needed money to continue his operation, and I invested quite a bit in the company. Eventually, I was the only investor, and my son Ben and I became directors. I owned four Clenet cars, two of each of the two models produced.

I started to become uncomfortable with the company's lawyer. I thought he was crooked, and told Alan Clenet so. Clenet insisted that he was in charge, and within a year, I caught Clenet making decisions I thought were suspect. As owner, I fired Clenet and liquidated the company.

Clenet Coachworks produced about 450 cars while I was involved with it. The product was well designed, but the lack of honesty destroyed the company. It's a sad story that I hope will serve as an example of the importance of integrity in business.

I later sued my own lawyer for settling the case without me and leaving me hanging alone. I hired another lawyer and the case was settled in my favor for $3.5 million.

HELPING OTHERS

MY ATTITUDE IS THIS: THE BEST PHILANTHROPY IS PERSONAL. Sure, you can give money away to an established cause or to an institution, and Helen and I certainly do. We give $1.5 million annually to schools, libraries, and other institutions of learning. But the greatest and most satisfying way to give, in my opinion, is very personally—giving money to a single individual you want to help.

There's a special satisfaction to be had from practicing personal acts of kindness. These needn't involve big sums of money. It might be just a little, but the thing that makes the giving special is that you know the individual who needs your help, or receives an unexpected gift. Over the years, I have helped young people around the world—often total strangers whom we met on our travels—come to the U.S., get a college education, get professional training, or just see parts of the world they would not have seen otherwise.

One night in 1963 I was in Bombay, India, at the Taj Mahal

Hotel, the same one that was bombed in 2009. The plane left at three in the morning, and I was sitting up, waiting for my departure. It was hot, and I felt like wandering around, so I went for a walk.

I counted 35 people resting on the stone floor of the Gateway to India. As I walked toward the sea, I saw three people sitting on a bench: a Muslim priest, his wife, and his daughter. He asked, in English, where I was from. We got to talking, and he introduced me to his family. "This is my daughter, Fatima. She goes to business college. She speaks English." She was 18 and indeed, spoke perfect English. I asked her if she'd ever wanted to come see America. Yes, she said, but her father was forbidden by law from sending money out of India. Before I left them, I took a photograph of us all.

At the time I was chairman of a women's college in Longmeadow, Massachusetts. I gave Fatima my card and told her, "Write me a letter if you'd like to come to the U.S."

Fatima wrote a couple of weeks later. "Mr. Blake, I am so sorry to hear about the assassination of your President Kennedy," she wrote. "I would like to come to Massachusetts and go to college." I persuaded the president of the college to give Fatima a $1,000 scholarship and I'd pay for the rest.

She came to the college and did very well. Fatima and her family became great friends with Helen and me. Many years later, Helen and I went to Bombay. We went to that same place where I'd first met Fatima's family, and we took another picture—Fatima and her father and Helen and me.

Fatima is married now, with two grown boys whom we helped put through dental school at Tufts. They live in Sacramento, in a big Muslim community there. We see Fatima or some of her family every couple of years or so when they come to visit us.

I'm not suggesting that the small amount of money I gave to Fatima and her family was better spent than if I'd given the same amount to the United Way or to any other big institutional charity.

But when you give very, very particularly, to a single individual, you get a special and different kind of benefit, a personal satisfaction. United Way isn't going to come stay with you at your home or send you pictures of its grandchildren.

Helen and I took a tour of England with a group of Rolls-Royce owners. We traveled with our cars overnight aboard ship and landed at Bilbao, Spain.

On our first day of driving, we pulled over to the side of the road to wait for some policemen to escort us through town. A couple and their daughter came up to see the cars. The girl, Arantxa Castillo, had a little dog in her arms. Her parents spoke only Spanish, but she spoke English. She was a very nice, clean-cut kind of gal—the kind of person you'd be proud to have for a granddaughter.

We started to chat. Before we left, I asked Arantxa if she'd like to visit the U.S. I told her I could find her volunteer jobs in the U.S. and she would be our guest. This was a fairy-tale kind of thing for her parents. But they were understandably skeptical. Should we let these strangers give our daughter a free trip? What do they want from us? I sent them an invitation to the dedication of the Blake Library in Florida to which Helen and I had contributed. That, along with a Christmas telephone call from our Spanish speaking son-in-law, seemed to help convince them that I was an upstanding guy and could afford to do this. Arantxa eventually came to visit. She spoke to her mother on the phone after she'd been here two days. "Oh, Mother," she said, "They've been so nice to me." That was over ten years ago, and we are still friends. She is like a granddaughter to us. She and her siblings have visited us several times since, and we have visited her family in Spain.

Remember the story of Army Private Jessica Lynch—the heroic servicewoman who was captured and so badly wounded during the 2003 Iraq war? I found her book, *I Am a Soldier, Too*, tremendously moving—so much so that I read it cover-to-cover three times. What was she up to today, I wondered? How is she now?

I reached her by telephone and invited her to visit Helen and me in Connecticut. Jessica and her parents came with her young daughter, Dakota Ann, a lovely little girl. They spent two and half days with us and we had a marvelous time. Jessica has had 22 operations, but she can walk now, drive a car, and go up and down stairs, though with a slight limp. Her ambition is to be a kindergarten teacher.

Helen and I did everything we could to make sure she and her family had a great visit with us. Dakota Ann loved swimming in the pool and feeding the fish in our pond. At day's end, we all ended up in a little rustic cottage on the property that is lighted by kerosene lamps. We laid a fire in the cabin's fireplace and ate our dinner by its glow. Afterwards we toasted marshmallows.

Jessica was so badly injured that even now she has to wear a brace on her left leg. But is she a crybaby? Not one bit. She's my idea of a hero.

One recipient of my personal philanthropy has been Northfield Mount Hermon School in Massachusetts. It's important to me because I attended prep school there (class of 1934, then called Mount Hermon School). My dad was class of 1904 and my son Ben was class of 1966. Curt's son Channing went there, too, as well as my grandchildren Maria Contos, and Christina, Andrew, and Juliana McCausland. I've committed several million dollars to the school because I believe in the education it offers young people. We've funded the building of Blake Hall, and given money for student scholarships. It's a school my family has attended and learned from, and I thought it was important to give back.

DeWitt Wallace, founder and head of Reader's Digest, taught me the right way to give money away to institutions.

You'd think you wouldn't have to learn that. You've been successful, you've been rewarded for your hard work, you want to share your good fortune with those less fortunate, so you pull out your checkbook and write a check. That's fine, as far as it goes. But I learned from Mr. Wallace that your gift goes farther if you give it in a way that challenges the recipient.

I recently made a challenge gift to the Wilbraham-Monson Academy, a school not far from our Friendly plant in Wilbraham, Massachusetts. I said I'd give them $1 million, provided they could match that with $3 million they would raise from their alumni and friends. Well, they did their part, and I did mine. Not only did the school get four million dollars, but you can be sure they'll use that money wisely. It's just like anything else: you value more highly the things you've had to work for. Four million dollars that you've had to earn is money you treat more respectfully than four million dollars that's just dumped in your lap. It's a fantastic way to give, for both the recipient and the giver alike.

PART 3

Back to *Friendly's*...

SOLD! TO MR. SMITH

ANOTHER THING I DID IN RETIREMENT WAS TO KEEP AN eye on Friendly.

I wanted "my baby" to be prosperous. From time to time I talked with some of the officers to find out how it was doing. Every August, I attended the Friendly's retiree's picnic. Whenever we were in Connecticut at Christmastime, dressed in my bow tie and blazer, I paid a visit to Friendly's manufacturing plant in Wilbraham to wish everybody there a happy holiday. I still do it occasionally, and I get a huge kick out of it. The truck drivers come up and give me a pat on the back. Some of the older ladies embrace me like a god returning from the dead. I seldom get away without a hug or a kiss.

In 1988, when Hershey sold the company to Donald Smith and a group of investors, the headline in *Nation's Restaurant News* (which turned out to be more prescient than its writers ever could have known) was: "Whiz-Kid Smith Takes a Whirl with Friendly." The press described Smith, aged 66, as a "fast-food wunderkind," and for good reason. At age 29, working for McDonald's, he'd risen to become the youngest field vice president in that company's history. In the 1970s, as Burger King's president, he'd doubled profits and turned the company around. Still later, as head of restaurants for PepsiCo, he increased profits 600% in two years.

Despite Smith's glowing resume, Hershey didn't want to sell when first approached about buying Friendly. But Smith persisted. Then-CEO Ken Wolf later told me that Hershey, in an effort to discourage Smith, had quoted a price so ridiculously high they never imagined he'd accept. To Hershey's surprise, Smith paid $375 million plus another $15 million in commissions. By my estimate, he overpaid by as much as $125 million. Biting off more than he could chew, however, turned out to be a Smith hallmark.

To finance the purchase, Smith put Friendly deeply into debt—something Curt and I had always been loath to do. Despite a 1997 sale of stock intended to help alleviate the financial pressure, Friendly's debt load swelled to an unwieldy and untenable $260 million.

The debt load of a company (or of an individual or of a nation) can only get so big before it becomes crushing. Interest costs begin to siphon money away from upkeep or training or new product development—activities essential to a business's life and health. This is what I saw happening at Friendly.

MELTING

AS THE 1990S DREW TO A CLOSE, I BEGAN TO HEAR DISTURBING reports from inside the company suggesting Friendly—by choice or by necessity—had begun to stray from some of the principles that for so long had been the underpinnings of its past success. I still had many friends who worked there, everybody from truck drivers to top management, and now and then I'd get a phone call or letter from someone concerned that things weren't quite right.

Nor were these insiders the only ones concerned.

Consumer Reports listed Friendly's dead last in a ranking of 18 national and regional family restaurant chains in a June 2000 article. *Restaurant Business* magazine served up an unappetizing picture of the company's situation in August 2000: Friendly was hobbled by $300 million in debt. Since the 1997 public offering, the company's share price had slid from a high of more than $25 to a low of $3 or less. Unit volume for the stores was down; profits were "woeful" (the magazine's word); the appearance of Friendly's restaurants was "worn out;" the service was "inconsistent." Friendly's prospects, wrote the magazine, were "as cold as its ice cream."

Around this time, I started getting unsolicited letters from total strangers, including ex-employees and customers, worried about Friendly's future. One came from a woman who had been trained as a Friendly's waitress in the 1960s. She was writing, she said, because she still felt "a certain loyalty" even though she no longer had any connection beyond being an occasional customer. She remembered the Friendly's she had worked for as a "tightly run ship" that prized cleanliness, low prices, and prompt service. The Friendly's of 2001, she said, had slipped. In the stores she and her friends patronized, she found tables stacked with dirty dishes, and employees making personal phone calls and visiting with one another when they should have been paying attention to customers' orders. Such shoddy standards, she noted, were "certainly not conducive" to Friendly's winning and keeping repeat business.

"I may not be a financial guru," she demurred, then went on to prescribe the solution to the problem. Friendly's needed to deliver better service, and to do that, it needed to invest more in training. With those improvements, she predicted, "the end result would be an increase in profits" and a reduction in the company's "encumbering debt." While this certainly hit home with me, her last words did even more so: "Friendly Ice Cream, as the name implies, should be a fun and friendly dining experience. It was built on this concept, but along the way this goal was lost."

She had put her finger on the problem better than any Wall Street analyst. Friendly had lost its way.

I received another letter—this one from a man who had been a Friendly manager. He said he was saddened to see Friendly on a "downward spiral." His analysis of the problem was strikingly similar to that of the former waitress: the discipline and principles that had guided our success were no longer being instilled. When he was a Friendly's manager, he wrote, competitors had tried to get him to sell them Friendly's training manual, so they could copy it and imitate our methods. "Of course I never did [sell it]," he wrote. "Today, however, an employee never sees a training manual. My daughter worked in a Friendly but she was never given more than a few hours training on the fountain and never had any follow-up training or progress reviews." Friendly, he said, had managed to turn "a silk purse" into "a sow's ear."

Mark Shachat, identifying himself as "a former employee," wrote a letter to the *Boston Globe* agreeing with a *Globe* piece by Brian McGrory. Shachat said that Friendly's service was slow in part because the menu—once a model of simplicity—had become "far too expansive." The store made famous by cones and burgers, McGrory wrote in his piece, was now peddling "fajitas, stir-fries, and quesadillas—none of it particularly well." Shachat remembered the Friendly's of the early 1980s as "a New England institution" known for great hamburgers, low prices, and attentive service, where customers enjoyed coming back again and again because the staff knew them by name. Now, he said, Friendly's was just another so-so restaurant chain in a crowded landscape, perched on verge of bankruptcy.

Friendly's management, of course, wasn't oblivious to this predicament, and steps were taken to improve results. In March 2000, Friendly announced it would close 150 of its 604 company-owned stores. Some were shuttered so abruptly—and with so little explanation—that customers, angry and surprised, were left to wonder if the whole company was closing up shop. More than 100 employees were laid off.

Still more new menu items were introduced, including soft serve ice cream and the Cyclone—a mix-in creation similar to today's Friend-Z—that allowed customers to mix Oreos, Heath Bars, M&M's, and other candies into their ice cream. Servers were given increased authority to address customer complaints right at the table, by issuing coupons or by offering free desserts and free meals. A new, re-designed prototype store was introduced.

All well and good, but the stock continued to languish. When it dipped below five dollars a share in mid-2000, the NASDAQ threatened to pull the company's listing, and Friendly, like an impoverished boarder forced to move to a shabbier hotel, relocated to the American Stock Exchange.

SAVING MY BABY

MY FRIEND LYMAN WOOD—A SHREWD INVESTOR IN ADDITION to being a successful business leader—told me he started buying Friendly stock when it was trading at around seven or eight dollars a share. I decided if Lyman Wood was buying, I ought to be, too. By Thanksgiving 2000, the price had fallen to $1.70, and I began to buy in 100,000-share lots. I had to buy aggressively if I were to bolster the price and thus help support my old company. *The New York Times* got wind of the story and wrote that Pres Blake, at age 86, was buying back his company. The item got quite a lot of play. My brother Curtis was riding in his car somewhere around Palm Beach, Florida, when he heard it on the radio. He was more surprised than anyone.

In just two weeks I owned almost 900,000 shares, much of it bought for under two dollars a share. This made me the largest single shareholder. In December I made a statement to reporters.

Perhaps things weren't so rosy just now at Friendly, I allowed, but I still believed in the company. "I won't say I'm going to work any miracles, but I am going to try. The big stockholders can take care of themselves. I'm doing this for the employees and the smaller stockholders who don't have any place else to go." As a sign of confidence in Friendly's future and as a gesture of goodwill, I announced I would sell, at some future date, 100,000 of my shares to Friendly employees at cost, no matter how high the price might have risen by then. I also donated about 250,000 shares to colleges and other deserving institutions, partly out of philanthropy, but also to keep my personal holdings under 10%. If you own in excess of 10% of a publicly traded company, the Securities and Exchange Commission considers you an insider. I most definitely wasn't an insider, as events soon would show.

My buying spree caught the attention of Donald Smith, Friendly's chairman and CEO—himself a big shareholder. Wouldn't I like to come visit him in his office in Memphis, he asked, to explain to him what my intentions were? It was Christmas, and I told him politely that I would not travel to Memphis for him or anybody else at that time. If he wanted to talk, I suggested, he could come to my winter home in Stuart, Florida.

In January 2001 he did just that.

Long before I met him, I knew there was plenty not to like about Don Smith. He had packed Friendly's board with yes-men, had saddled Friendly with crushing debt, and had presided over the free fall of its stock from $25 to $1.70 a share. He seemed to me to be the very worst kind of executive.

Despite his impressive list of whiz-kid accomplishments (or maybe because of them), he had acquired an attitude of imperial entitlement. He lived large at shareholder expense, flitting hither and thither aboard a corporate jet. I didn't see how it made financial sense for Friendly to even own a jet, let alone for it to be used as the personal plaything of the CEO. Our restaurants weren't spread far and wide around the world. The majority of them were concentrated in the Northeast. Smith, in my opinion, could just as easily have conducted business using commercial airlines, at a far lower cost to shareholders.

His style of management was to browbeat subordinates with foul language. Anyone who challenged him was threatened with dismissal. And he was capable of a kind of meanness so petty as to be, well, just about unbelievable. I enjoyed—and Friendly employees enjoyed—my annual visit to the Wilbraham plant at Christmas. Once Smith decided I was the enemy, he told me that if he wanted, he could get a restraining order to keep me away. The Friendly plant was private property. The very idea! I was frosted.

On top of everything else, Smith played golf, and many of his jet rides were to go from one tournament to another, not for company business.

Don Smith and Friendly's president John Cutter arrived at my house in Florida via the corporate jet to chat. When they had settled into chairs in our solarium, I was taken aback to see that Smith had brought along a tape recorder, with which he intended to record our conversation. This did not strike me as particularly friendly—certainly not the act of a well-intentioned man who had nothing to hide. But thank goodness for that recorder! I am sure he planned to use anything I might say against me. Ironically, it was Smith's own comments, captured on that tape, that later cost him.

He asked what my plans were, and I told him, as diplomatically as I could, that for the good of the company I felt he should step aside and let others take over.

His pleasant and cordial response was that John Cutter was running the company now, and that he (Smith) was only going to the office about two days a month. At a time when he was being paid by Friendly upwards of half a million dollars a year in salary and bonus, he said, with the tape running: "I don't spend hardly any time at Friendly's anymore. I go in two days a month, I go to board meetings, I'm available and we talk once or twice a week on the phone, but make no doubt about it—I really do not run Friendly's anymore."

We talked for another hour or so about company operations. I was delighted to think that there was apparently going to be no confrontation, which I had wanted to avoid. As I took him back to the airport, we had a pleasant conversation about what a wonderful job each of us had done in our business (neither one of us, of course, being the least bit sincere). I purposely did not go out to the jet, so great an irritation had it become to me. I did not want to even look at it.

After Smith left, I hired a detective to do some checking up on him. I made sure Smith knew that I was investigating him, to throw him off balance and make him nervous. We found he had multiple homes. His house in Naples, Florida, had a $2.8 million mortgage, which made me think he was living beyond his means. His home in Chicago was in his wife's name, which struck me as something you'd do if you feared your creditors might some day come knocking.

As winter became spring, my dissatisfaction with Smith deepened. I resolved to confront him at Friendly's May 2001 annual meeting.

Our confrontation was the opening shot in what would become a war, and the first public inkling that a struggle was to begin. That it would become the stuff of a Harvard Business School case study, with implications for American corporate governance, I don't think I or anyone else at the time imagined.

Nor did I imagine my fight for justice would bring about the estrangement of my brother and me.

Curt felt I was in the wrong to go after Smith, and he said

so publicly in an op-ed piece in our hometown newspaper, the *Springfield Republican*. Curt wrote that Don Smith had done only good things since buying Friendly. These included mounting a strong defense against my "insistent bashing." He dismissed my proposed solutions for Friendly's troubles as being "of no value." Curt then got personal, asserting that by my actions I had "alienated much of the Blake family" and had created "a rift that can never be healed." I don't have to tell you this was a bitter thing to hear from my own brother and business partner of 43 years.

Despite Curt's harsh words, I pressed on, zeroing in on Smith's use of the corporate jet—in particular his use of it for non-business and family travel. He promised to produce checks showing that he had reimbursed Friendly for such use. But he didn't. Instead, Friendly's board appointed a special committee to conduct an in-house investigation to determine if Smith's use of the plane had been in any way improper. But Smith himself named an employee as the head of that investigation—a man whose compensation was determined by Smith! The head of the investigation was being asked, in effect, to investigate his own boss. Not surprisingly, the committee determined there had been no wrongdoing.

In addition to his improper personal conduct, Smith was selling off valuable assets and real estate, including 200 Friendly stores and Friendly's Troy, Ohio plant.

Rather than show its impartiality and independence, the board did Smith's bidding at every turn, never challenging him. Why? It's probably not irrelevant that they all were receiving, from Smith, unusually high pay. I was a stockholder of J.P. Morgan Bank, so I knew what fees were being paid to Morgan's directors. It was less than what Friendly's directors got, and Morgan was a more solvent and far bigger business. In my opinion, Smith's loyalty from the Friendly's directors had been bought. A former Friendly officer once said it to me this way: the only friends Smith had were the ones he'd paid for.

I got tired of being stonewalled by the board and Smith. So, on the advice of my attorney, James Donnelly of Mirick, O'Connell in Worcester, Massachusetts, I went to court. *Blake v. Friendly Ice Cream Corp.*, filed January 2, 2003, alleged breach of fiduciary duty and misappropriation of corporate assets, primarily Smith's use of the airplane. The type of suit we filed is a derivative action, brought on behalf of a company and its shareholders. In such suits, any money damages awarded go to the company and its shareholders, not to the individual who brings the suit. All he gets, if he's lucky, is reimbursement for his legal expenses.

Jim worked hard filing papers and taking depositions. It was all very time consuming, and costs quickly mounted. Because I wanted Jim to put his best efforts into the case, I made sure all my legal bills were paid within two or three days of receipt, which was always two or three weeks before their due date. Jim once told me I was the fastest paying client his firm ever had.

The legal maneuverings on both sides were complicated and protracted, but slowly we gained ground.

Instead of addressing the issues we'd raised, Smith and his lawyers moved to have our suit dismissed on a technicality. When this motion came up for a hearing, the Superior Court judge told Friendly he would take no action until they produced the airplane records we had been seeking—logs and other documents showing who had used the plane when, and for what purposes. The judge didn't just deny Friendly's motion, he rebuked its board for having conducted an investigation "so lacking in substance" as to "raise serious questions about the good faith and reasonableness" of the inquiry.

The logs, when produced, showed that my suspicions had been well founded: Smith had used the jet to attend golf tournaments, for family travel, and for other personal purposes.

In the discovery phase of the suit, we began to find evidence of other, more serious ethical lapses and of other forms of misappropriation.

Smith's business interests included a holding company, Tennessee Restaurant Company (TRC), through which he and his associates had purchased Friendly in 1988. TRC also owned 100% of the Perkins family restaurant chain. After Friendly's issuance of stock in 1997, Smith himself owned just 10% of Friendly but 70% of TRC. That meant every dollar siphoned from Friendly to Perkins (and every cost shifted from the latter to the former) stood to make Smith a richer man.

Through our research, and by comparing the SEC filings for Friendly with those for TRC, we discovered the following:

- Friendly had failed to disclose that two of its directors had also been directors of TRC.
- Related party transactions had not been properly disclosed: Friendly was paying substantial amounts of money to TRC but getting only a questionable return. For example, although TRC was enjoying more than half the use of the corporate jet, Friendly was paying half its cost.
- There was no written agreement between Friendly and TRC that required Friendly to share the aircraft costs.
- There was a $2.1 million accounting discrepancy between what Friendly said it had paid to TRC and what TRC said it had received.
- A division of TRC, Foxtail Foods, acted as the purchaser of food supplies for both Friendly and Perkins. Between 1998 and 2004, Friendly paid Foxtail between $4.4 and $5.3 million, though there was no evidence to show that Foxtail had ever competitively bid for Friendly's business.

- Smith's two sons had enjoyed what appeared to be preferential treatment in their acquisition of a Friendly's franchise.
- Our estimates showed TRC owed Friendly something on the order of $12 million.

Friendly's response in 2004 was to conduct a second internal "special investigation," which again sidestepped the important issues. But the board, knowing that for appearance's sake it could not let Smith off scot-free, told him to reimburse the company $70,000 for his personal use of company aircraft. After that, Friendly's lawyers moved a second time to dismiss our suit.

Their motion to dismiss was the biggest challenge we had faced up to that point, in part because the special committee had hired forensic accountants for its investigation and a top-rate law firm. Nevertheless, our main contention remained that Friendly's board and the special committee had failed to exercise independent judgment.

It happens that in Massachusetts at this time, board independence was a very lively issue. In fact, it was a cutting-edge issue nationwide, in such cases as the Walt Disney derivative suit and the Oracle derivative investigation.

Justice was done in May 2006. The judge, in a landmark 50-page decision, put his finger on the issue. The problem at Friendly, he found, was that the board was incapable of exercising independent judgment. He found further that the board's internal investigations had not been in good faith. "[The] investigation was so lacking in substance, scope and support as to raise serious questions about the good faith and reasonableness of the...inquiry." Nor did he spare the individual directors. Director Burton J. Manning, for example, was found "largely oblivious to his obligations." Of director Steven L. Ezzes he wrote: "Ezzes' deposition testimony was marked by evasion, surliness and memory loss and portrays a stunning degree of ignorance, whether feigned or real, about the transactions material to the plaintiff's allegations." Rather than dismiss our suit, the judge ordered that more evidence be produced. We were elated!

In June 2006 we got a huge boost from a story that appeared in *The Wall Street Journal.* Writer John Hechinger spent nearly three months investigating it, and the result was accurate and well written. It detailed the differences between Smith and me and depicted the board of directors as anything but independent.

One person who read the story was Sardar Biglari, a 29-year-old investor 2,000 miles away in Texas, who shared many of my concerns about Friendly as well as my optimism that the company could be put right. He and his partner Philip Cooley had been watching Friendly, and, through their company, the Lion Hedge Fund, increased their purchase of shares to give them almost 15% ownership. They asked Smith for two seats on the Friendly board, which he at first refused. They began to entertain the idea of waging a proxy fight.

Now there arose a host of problems and complications, the combined effect of which was to frustrate efforts by me, Biglari, and other parties to unseat Friendly management.

One issue was an SEC provision forbidding big shareholders from joining forces if, together, they owned more than 15% of a company. Another was the fact that Friendly had a "staggered" board—meaning only two directors could come up for election in any one year. On top of that, some of the company's loans had been structured in such a way as to become due immediately if and when shareholders changed control of the company. These and other "poison pills"—stratagems by management to entrench itself—had become a common (if deplorable) feature of corporate governance.

I decided nonetheless to move ahead, independent of Biglari and other shareholders. I knew Smith was almost as desperate to avoid a proxy fight as he was to escape my lawsuit. So I started buying stock again in March 2007, picking up another 250,000 shares at $10 to $12 a share in a few days—enough for Smith to see that there was no way that he could now prevail.

Smith and his directors at last bowed to the inevitable. They postponed the May 2007 annual meeting and instead announced they had retained Goldman Sachs to find a buyer for the company. After a few anxious weeks and several overtures from potential buyers, they got a solid offer of $15.50 a share from Sun Capital of Boca Raton, Florida.

It was an offer that seemed acceptable to just about everyone but me. On the one hand, $15.50 was a windfall for shareholders, including the Friendly retirees I'd set out to protect. But on the other hand, Sun's acquisition would let Smith and the board off the hook, since a derivative lawsuit ends in the event of a merger or an acquisition.

It was a situation that presented me with a terrible dilemma. Even though the court's various decisions had already achieved a measure of justice by putting on record the ethical lapses of the board and Smith, the defendants would be saved from any further accountability. If I refused to vote in favor of the settlement, the legal fight would go on, with no guarantee our side would prevail or that Friendly shareholders would see their investment saved. What was I to do?

Just when I thought the pressure to act could not get any worse, Sun Capital upped the ante by saying it would withdraw its offer unless I voted for the merger with all my shares. This prevented me from keeping my promise to sell 100,000 shares to employees at my cost.

In the end, I voted in favor. Much as I wanted to see Smith and certain members of the board get their comeuppance, the value of the merger to the company and its shareholders was immense.

The sale, consummated August 31, 2007, had cost me seven years to achieve—not to mention $11 million of my own money. To pay the bills I'd had to sell some of my beloved Rolls-Royces. That hurt, of course. But as I told a reporter early in the fight, "When you get a bad disease, the medicine is bitter, bitter, bitter." As far as I was concerned, it had all been worth it. I'd done what I'd set out to do—remove Smith and his directors so that Friendly was free to be managed by people better qualified to increase its value and chart its future.

I couldn't quibble when my hometown newspaper in Springfield reported that those on the Pres Blake side of this most unfriendly war were now enjoying "a sundae with three cherries on top."

Much to my surprise, the Harvard Business School found the whole story of our fight for justice to be so compelling that in April 2008 they wrote it up as a 30-page case study, its lessons for tomorrow's business leaders. It was a great satisfaction to me to be present at the first teaching of it. There was a standing ovation from the faculty and the 75 students in the class at the end of my participation. What better swan song in business could a man have?

On a very personal note, I am happy to relate that my brother and I eventually healed our rift, and that the two of us are now speaking civilly again to one another.

When the dust had settled, I took out an advertisement in the *Republican* to list what I thought I had accomplished. I had saved the retirement investment of Friendly's many small shareholders; I had brought about the ouster of persons shown to have been up to no good; I had helped assure the continuation of the high ethical principles on which Friendly was founded; and I had helped restore Friendly's strong financial standing.

The *Republican* did its own summing up. It called the resolution "good news for shareholders and the future of the company" and "good news for the 400 people employed at the company's Wilbraham headquarters." The newspaper's editorial ended with this: "Pres Blake...has always had the best interests of Friendly's—and its employees—at heart. His perseverance has paid off." I'd like to think that somewhere Mr. Penney was smiling down on me for a job well done. Friendly now was ready, once again, to be both ethical and profitable.

Today I no longer own any Friendly stock. I don't have any official involvement with the company at all. I'm just a retired co-founder. But I love to make my Christmas visit when the weather allows. And every summer I still attend Friendly's annual retiree's picnic, where, you can be sure, I eat my share of ice cream.

Epilogue

WHAT I TELL KIDS

MY ADVICE FOR ANYBODY STARTING OUT IN LIFE IS SIMPLE: get to work! Learn the nitty-gritty.

Start a business like Curt and I did. Or get a job in a successful company that peddles the kind of thing you're interested in. See how they do it on the inside. Years ago, somebody starting out in business might have swept floors. Today, you can work as a programmer or a summer intern. Either way, if you keep your eyes open and pay attention, you'll see what they are doing right. You'll see the mistakes. You'll see how and where the business is expanding, developing, and where opportunities might lie.

You might be just pushing papers around, but the boss is working over there, and you can see how he or she works, talks to people, and handles situations. It's a good way to get started: associate yourself with someone who is already a success. Don't waste your time with somebody who's just shuffling money or changing dollars and not producing anything. You can't create real wealth without production.

Make sure you learn the basics of your business, whichever one you pick. My father said to me, "If you study a business, learn all the phases of it, and apply what you learn intelligently. You can't help but be successful." And he was right. I did that in the ice cream business. I learned how a refrigeration compressor works. I learned how to lay out a store, so that the people in it can work with maximum efficiency. I learned how much fat ice cream needs to have—how much is too much, how much is too little, how much is just right. Milk from Jersey cows has the most fat right out of the cow, and milk from Holsteins has the least. The higher the fat in ice cream, the "warmer" it tastes on your tongue, even though all ice cream is the same temperature.

And if you're going to scoop ice cream, don't dribble! It drives me crazy to see a clerk take a scoop out of a well of cold water and then dribble water drops into the ice cream as he's scooping. No! For every drop of water that falls, you get a piece of ice in the ice cream. Shake the scoop free of water, then scoop.

No matter what business you go into, never hesitate to ask advice from the most senior and successful leaders. They're never too big or too busy to share advice with young, ambitious people who approach them with sincerity and respect. Remember the reception I got from J.C. Penney, Harlow Curtice, Tom Murphy, and other prominent people who were willing to help the young, struggling Blake brothers.

And one more important thing for young people to remember: no smoking, no liquor, and no drugs! I've never smoked. When I turned 18, my parents said, "Smoking is your decision. But if you want to smoke, you'll have to find somewhere else to live." So I never started. And I don't enjoy the taste of beer, wine, or the hard stuff. Besides, it's very expensive!

So that's my story. I started small, worked hard, and succeeded beyond my wildest dreams. I got out of the ice cream business and was sitting pretty until I had to get off the couch and back into the fray.

That battle's over. I'm 96 and I'm officially retired.

Maybe.

ABOUT THE AUTHORS

S. Prestley Blake, at age 96, divides his time between homes in Florida and Connecticut, enjoys visits from his many friends around the world, still sails occasionally, and still dabbles in Rolls-Royces. He loves hearing from former employees. Every August he attends the retiree's picnic, and occasionally, dressed jauntily in bow tie and blazer, he pays a visit to Friendly's manufacturing plant in Wilbraham, Massachusetts. Pres and his wife Helen support many causes, giving away $1.5 million a year. He especially enjoys speaking to audiences of young people, telling them that they, too, can enjoy a successful life if they work hard and play by the rules.

Alan Farnham is currently covering business stories for ABCNews.com. He previously worked for *Forbes* magazine as senior editor, overseeing lifestyle coverage. Prior to that he was a senior writer at *Fortune* for 13 years. His books include *Guts: The Seven Laws of Business That Made Chrysler the World's Hottest Car Company* (John Wiley & Sons, 1998), ghost-written for Chrysler's then-vice chairman Robert Lutz; and *Forbes Great Success Stories: Twelve Tales of Victory Wrested from Defeat* (John Wiley & Sons, 2000), written under his own byline.